A Concise Greek Grammar

A Concise Greek Grammar

First English Edition

Jamin Andreas Hübner

Hills Publishing Group • Rapid City, South Dakota

A Concise Greek Grammar
Copyright ©2018 Jamin Andreas Hübner
All Rights Reserved.
Printed in the United States of America
First English Edition

Hills Publishing Group
Rapid City, South Dakota
hillspublishinggroup@protonmail.com

ISBN (13-digit): 978-0-9905943-4-5
ISBN (10-digit): 0990594343

Unless otherwise noted, all biblical quotations are from the *New Revised Standard Version Bible*, copyright 1989, Division of Christian Education of the Natonal Council of the Churches of Christ in the United States of America. Used by permission. All rights reserved.

Cover photo by Jamin Andreas Hübner, the "Madaba Map" in Madaba, Jordan (taken January 11, 2013 at Saint George Byzantine Orthodox Church)

For "Father Kobes"
(Professor Wayne Kobes)

And special thanks to…
The Greek classes of 2012-17 at John Witherspoon College, for letting me test-drive this work on their poor souls,
and for all those humble exegetical commentators whose labor will never be fully appreciated.

CONTENTS

Abbreviations 8
Preface to the First English Edition 11

Section I: Noun System
1. Alphabet, Pronunciation, and Punctuation 30
2. First and Second Declension Nouns 46
3. Articles, Prepositions, and Third Declension Nouns 65
4. Adjectives and Adverbs 78
5. Personal Pronouns 87
6. Demonstrative and Relative Pronouns 95

Section II: Verb System
7. Intro to Verbs and Present Active Indicative 102
8. Present Middle/Passive and Contract Verbs 114
9. Imperfect and εἰμί 122
10. Future Active/Middle and Stem/Root Changes 129
11. Future Passive and Aorist 142
12. Perfect and PluPerfect 155
13. Subjunctive and Infinitive 165
14. Imperative and μι Verbs 174

Section III: Participles
15. Introduction to Participles and Present Participles 179
16. Simple and Perfect Participles 185

17. Practical Reasons for Learning New Testament Greek 193

Grammatical Glossary 209

ABBREVIATIONS

abbr.	abbreviation
acc.	accusative
act.	active
adj.	adjective
adv.	adverb
alt.	alternate/alternative
aor.	aorist
art.	article
BBG	*Basics of Biblical Greek* (2009)
BDAG	Bauer, Danker, Arndt, Gingrich, *A Greek-English Lexicon of the New Testament* (2000)
c.	circa, about
CEB	Commen English Bible
CEV	Century English Version
CL	*The Concise Greek-English Lexicon of the New Testament* (2009)
cog.	cognate
dat.	dative
DBL	*A Dictionary of Biblical Languages: Greek* (2001)
def.	definition/definite
dem.	demonstrative
e.g.,	*exempli gratia*, for example
esp.	especially
f.	and verse following
ff.	and verses following
fem.	feminine
freq.	frequently
fut.	future

ESV	English Standard Version
gen.	genitive
GGBB	*Greek Grammar Beyond the Basics* (1998)
Heb.	Hebrew
Hübner	Author's (Hübner's) translation/rendering
i.e.,	*id est*, it is, that is
IGEL	*An Intermediate Greek-English Lexicon* (1945)
ind.	indicative
indef.	indefinite
inf.	infinitive
impf.	imperfect
impv.	imperative
KJV	King James Version
LXX	Septuagint
masc.	masculine
ms.	manuscript
mss.	manuscripts
n.	noun
NA26	Nestle-Aland 26th Edition
NA27	Nestle-Aland 27th Edition
NA28	Nestle-Aland 28th Edition
NASB	New American Standard Bible (1995 ed.)
NET	New English Translation
NIV	New International Version (2011 ed.)
NLT	New Living Translation (2nd ed.)
nom.	nominative
NRSV	New Revised Standard Version
NT	New Testament
obj.	object
OT	Old Testament
pass.	passive
pf.	perfect

pl.	plural
pos.	positive
poss.	posessive
ppos.	post-positive
prep.	preposition
pres.	present
prim.	primarily
pron.	pronoun
ptc.	participle
reflex.	reflexive
RSV	Revised Standard Version
sg.	singular
subj.	subject
suff.	suffix
TNIV	Today's New International Version
trad.	traditionally
temp.	temporal
UBS	United Bible Society
UBS4	United Bible Society Greek NT, 4th Edition
UBS5	United Bible Society Greek NT, 5th Edition
v.	verse/verb
vv.	verses
w.	with

Preface to the First English Edition

Introduction

After the last few years of drowning in academic research, I've often said three things to myself: "The last thing we[1] need is another Bible translation," and "the last thing we need is another commentary series," and finally, "the last thing we need is another Greek grammar." And yet, despite the publishing madness of our age, you now hold a new Greek grammar in your hands. What defense can be made? It is not as if there are no alternatives, such as Mounce,[2] Black,[3] Dobson,[4] Summers-Sawyer,[5] Smith-Fullmer,[6] Porter,[7] Davis,[8] Mare,[9] Decker,[10] Campbell and

---

[1] I.e., English-speaking Christians.
[2] William Mounce, *The Basics of Biblical Greek* (Grand Rapids: Zondervan, 2009).
[3] David Black, *Learn to Read New Testament Greek* (Nashville: Broadman and Holman, 2009).
[4] John Dobson, *Learn New Testament Greek* (Grand Rapids: Baker, 1989).
[5] Ray Summers and Thomas Sawyer, *Essentials of New Testament Greek* (Nashville: Broadman and Holman, 1995).
[6] Robert Smith and Paul Fullmer, *Read Greek by Friday* (Eugene: Wipf and Stock, 2004).
[7] Stanley Porter, Jeffrey Reed, Matthew O'Donnell, *Fundamentals of New Testament Greek* (Grand Rapids: Eerdmans, 2010).

Gibson,[11] and classics like Goodwin[12] and Machen.[13] There is a Greek grammar for virtually every type of student and situation imaginable.[14]

In the first draft of this preface, I tried to address this concern in full to students and teachers. But that project alone proved far too cumbersome. Instead, I can only summarize (mainly for teachers) how this work differs from alternatives and say "just give it a try, and you'll see."

How, then, does this grammar differ from the others? Below is a handful of some of the most distinctive variances (in no particular order).

How This Work is Different

First of all, students are required to learn how to pronounce Greek as it was (most likely) originally spoken during the Koiné Greek era, a pronunciation system often called "Restored Koiné."

---

[8] William Davis, *Beginner's Grammar of the Greek New Testament* (Eugene: Wipf and Stock, 2005).
[9] W. Mare, *Mastering New Testament Greek* (Grand Rapids: Baker, 1975), republished in 2001 by Wipf and Stock.
[10] Rodney Decker, *Reading Koine Greek* (Grand Rapids: Baker Academic, 2014).
[11] Constantine Campbell and Richard Gibson, *Reading Biblical Greek* (Grand Rapids: Zondervan, 2017).
[12] William Goodwin, *A Greek Grammar* (Tiger Xenophone, 1892, 2008).
[13] John Machen, *New Testament Greek for Beginners* (New York: Pearson, 2003).
[14] For what it's worth, I consider Decker and Porter to be of the highest quality in this list of alternatives.

Preface to the First Edition

This may come as a surprise to many readers, but this is not how *any* Greek textbook (to my knowledge) approaches the matter.[15]

The authentic pronunciation of Koiné Greek has (and probably never will be) decisively established.[16] However, there has been considerable progress in recent times—enough progress to the point of resconsidering the pedagogic implications for textbooks like this one. There have been competing theories of how Greek was originally pronounced ever since Erasmus's work on the subject in the 16th century.[17] Eventually, this gap in knowledge,

---

[15] The closest exception is Decker and Campbell, who includes both the Erasmian and the Restored pronunciation. Decker in *Reading*, xxi, intentionally chooses not to adopt the Restored pronunciation, saying, "Personally, I use a traditional Erasmian system, freely acknowledging that it is not an accurate representation of exactly what Jesus and Paul sounded like when they spoke Greek." No further explanation is given for this choice, though I assume it is simply because of convenience and trend-related pressures.
Porter et. al., *Fundamentals*, 4, interestingly includes the Modern Greek pronunciation in addition to the American Erasmian. Decker rightly responds to this approach by saying, "Modern Greek pronunciation…is anachronistic and certainly not accurate, though it may be closer to Koine than Erasmian." More significant, the authors err in saying that the Erasmian system "follows the scheme of the Renaissance scholar Erasmus," when in fact the current Erasmian system they present (the American Erasmian) is a *corruption* of Erasmus's original pronunciation system. In the words of Schwandt, "Erasmus' own arguments can be leveled against the 'Erasmian' pronunciation. Unfortunately, the reconstructed historical pronunciation isn't the one that bears his name." See John Schwandt, "Guide to Greek Pronunciation Conventions." *Institute of Biblical Greek*. http://www.biblicalgreek.org/links/pronunciation.php (accessed July 6, 2015).

[16] See Decker, *Reading*, xxi; ch 1.

[17] Mounce, *BBG*, 7, vastly understates the situation: "There is some disagreement as to the correct pronunciation of a few of the letters…" He continues, "I have chosen the standard pronunciations that will help you learn the language the easiest." This misleads students not only with regard to the nature of what is historically "standard" (cf. p. 8, n. 4, 6), but suggests that pronunciation is simply not part of learning "the language." With Porter (see *Fundamentals*, xiv) and other

combined with the immediate need to make pronunciation and teaching of Greek easier for English-speakers,[18] forged artificial systems of pronunciation that *sort of* reflected ancient Greek and *sort of reflected* Modern Greek, but did not reflect how anyone actually spoke the language at *any* time in history. Regrettably, the most popular of these novel systems, the American (or U.S.) Erasmian system, remains the default in most biblical-studies circles to this day.[19]

Many grammarians do not consider pronunciation a significant issue because correct pronunciation is not required for correct reading (and translation).[20] But this dismissive attitude also originates from the centuries of ambiguity regarding pronunciation and the potential implications of its revision. Few people like admitting that they spent years of their life learning (or decades of their life teaching!) how to *incorrectly* pronounce a language—much less admitting how this might be detrimental to students' education.

It is true that there is limited importance in correct (or even remotely correct) pronunciation. But this should be not reason to overlook several vital features of learning a language—especially if one is to teach and learn a language effectively. *Hearing* words is perhaps the most effective way at mastering vocabulary. This is why digital/app Greek flash cards often include audio

---

grammarians, I beg to differ—especially given the oral nature of languages in general, and of Koiné in particular.

[18] For example, U.S. Erasmian pronunciation of ει, αι, and οι matches the common English diphthongs ei, ai, and oi.

[19] I do not know how Europeans typically pronounce Greek in their classes, but I would suspect it would be Erasmian or strictly Modern.

[20] E.g., Decker, *Reading*, xxii, says "If you were learning to *speak* Greek (either Koine or modern), then pronunciation would obviously be far more important."

pronunciation. This is also why I, like other professors, require students to say their vocabulary words outloud as they study.[21] Students remember how words sound, not simply how they appear and are spelled. And words pronounced as people actually speak (or spoke) them are more natural and smooth in their flow, and can thereby assist in memorization. For the same reason, closer pronunciation to genuine Koiné Greek makes classroom readings easier and less choppy. One only has to visit the Biblical Languages Center website[22] and listen to the New Testament audio readings, and then compare them with, for example, the audio readings of William Mounce.[23] The difference is night and day.

Grammarians who are aware of this problem make additional excuses for continuing to teach incorrect pronunciation. To use one example, William Mounce says, "I follow the standard pronunciation of Koine Greek (also called 'Erasmian'). There is increasing interest in modern Greek pronunciation...But the majority of students learn the standard pronunciation, and those who learn modern [or Restored] often have difficulty communicating with students from other schools."[24] Possibly. But does this potential difficulty really warrant another generation of Christian scholars and pastors who pronounce Greek in a way that no one in history pronounced it? Is following such a tradition worth the potentially long-term cost? And, more importantly, should students just uncritically accept what is considered "standard" (and the implication that consensus somehow makes it

---

[21] Cf. Porter et. al., *Fundamentals,* xiv: "We like to emphasize pronunciation..."
[22] www.biblicallanguagecenter.com.
[23] https://www.teknia.com.
[24] *BBG,* xi.

more "right")? These are questions professors should be asking—and encouraging their students to ask as well.[25]

Second, this text implements the vocabulary and vocabulary categories from perhaps the most respected and widely used Greek-English Lexicon, *BDAG*.[26] Strangely, many grammars to do not even identify where they are getting their vocabulary definitions from! Like pronunciation, there are plenty of (misleading) claims about "standard vocabulary" or "traditional definitions," but this is often a cover for "the vocabulary I used as a student back in my seminary days (and I don't care to change)," or "*my personally-preferred* definitions," or simply the "theologically-correct" definitions of the day. The result is that one of the most crucial aspects of learning Greek (vocabulary) is disconnected from the best resources available and enslaved to the biases of one or two grammarians or grammatical schools. Students inevitably end up spending countless hours learning a set of definitions only to have to unlearn them a few years later

---

[25] I can't help but notice the parallel between this kind of argumentation and ideologies like King James Onlyism, where we are essentially told (to use Mounce's same phrasing), "I use the standard Bible translation (the 'KJV'). There is increasing interest in modern translations like the NIV and NRSV...But the majority of folks use the standard translation, and those who learn from the NIV and NRSV often have difficulty communicating with Christians from other churches." Hopefully one can see the problems with this kind of approach. As if it needed to be stated, the modern translations are now the default for most Christians, at least for those with academic interests. (I hope the same will happen with Koiné Greek pronunciation.)

[26] Walter Bauer, Frederick Danker, William Arndt, F. Gingrich, *A Greek-English Lexicon of the New Testament and Other Early Christian Literature* (Chicago: University of Chicago Press, 2000). More precisely, the vocabulary comes from the condensed version of *BDAG*, Frederick Danker, *The Concise Greek-English Lexicon of the New Testament* (Chicago: University of Chicago Press, 2009).

Preface to the First Edition

when they enter more advanced study. This is utterly unnecessary.

This sorry state of affairs is no exaggeration. The first draft of this grammar used Mounce's vocabulary definitions, but for the reasons mentioned above, I decided to switch to those in the Danker's *Concise Lexicon* (from *BDAG*). This process of revision was fascinating to me as I was able to systematically witness first hand just how much the two vocabulary databases varied. Initially, I assumed they would be 95% alike.

As it turned out, *they were about 95% different*. The revisions were considerable (additions, substitutions, subtractions), many of which involved a completely new set of glosses without any resemblance to Mounce's entries. Clearly, *BDAG* was not being followed—and, as far as I could tell, neither was any other single lexicon. There was no clearly-defined reason as to why certain definitions/glosses were used and not others.[27]

It is no wonder that Mounce himself expressed regret over this fact in 2013: "Part of my frustration…is making me think about the glosses we memorize. They are necessarily short due to the needs of first year Greek, but shouldn't we be memorizing more complete meanings that reflect semantic range in our second year?"[28] Second year? Why not the first? I see no reason to have students re-learn an entire set of Greek vocabulary![29]

---

[27] This is not to say that grammarians do not have their reasons, or that some definitions and variants from *BDAG* are not warranted. (To use on example, the addition of "mutually" to Danker's glosses of ajllhvlwn appears appropriate).

[28] Bill Mounce, "Does Jesus always do things "immediately" (Monday with Mounce 175)." *ZondervanAcademic.com*. (February 13, 2013).

[29] I asked my students if they would prefer to do this. My ear still hurts from the response.

The same is true for other grammars. If there is something to be said about unformity and "standardization," then it would make sense to at least have students memorize the vocabulary (and basic semantic categories) from a lexicon that they will likely be using for the rest of their adult lives. This is what I have done—in addition to *excluding* a lexicon from the back of the book. Students are therefore encouraged to get familiar with the "right" resources right away, which saves them all the more work down the road.

On to a third difference. Special attention is payed to visual memorization, especially with regard to tables and charts. It has been proven in various educational and psychological contexts that shapes are typically easier to memorize than plains text. In political technology, for example, it unwise to use all-capital letters for a name tag, because all-caps eliminate the unique shape of a person's name (thereby making it harder for people to remember). The same goes for memorizing paradigms and tables.

To put this into perspective, observe the the table of noun case endings in two Greek textbooks[30]:

---

[30] Mounce, *BBG*, 45 and Porter et. al., *Fundamentals*, 23. Decker tries to be more progressive by adding shaded backgrounds to certain columns, but it is still far from visually-effective.

Preface to the First Edition

	2 *masc*	1 *fem*	2 *neut*
nom sg	ς	–	ν
gen sg	ῡ	ς	ῡ
*dat sg*⁷	ι	ι	ι
acc sg	ν	ν	ν
nom pl	ι	ι	α
gen pl	ων	ων	ων
dat pl	ις	ις	ις
acc pl	υς	ς	α

Second Declension Noun Endings		
	Masc./Fem.	Neut.
Singular Nom.	**-ος**	**-ον**
Voc.	**-ε**	**-ον**
Gen.	**-ου**	**-ου**
Dat.	**-ῳ**	**-ῳ**
Acc.	**-ον**	**-ον**
Plural Nom.	**-οι**	**-α**
Gen.	**-ων**	**-ων**
Dat.	**-οις**	**-οις**
Acc.	**-ους**	**-α**

As you can see, there is no particular shapes by which student can memorize the (similar or different) contents of the table. Compare this with table of case endings used in this grammar:

	2nd	1st	2nd	3rd	
	Masc	Fem	Neut	M/F	Neut
Sg Nom	ς	–	ν	ς / –	–
Sg Gen	υ	ς	υ	ος	ος
Sg Dat	ι	ι	ι	ι	ι
Sg Acc	ν	ν	ν	α / ν	–
Pl Nom	ι	ι	α	ες	α
Pl Gen	ων	ων	ων	ων	ων
Pl Dat	ις	ις	ις	σι(ν)	σι(ν)
Pl Acc	υς	ς	α	ας	α

The major difference (other than the obvious inclusion of third-declension endings) is the consolidation of borders for the same endings. This make memorization considerably easier— especially on tests and workbooks that present an empty table. Using the first model above, students would be given nothing but a blank space to fill. In the second, here is what they see:

Preface to the First Edition

	2ⁿᵈ	1ˢᵗ	2ⁿᵈ	3ʳᵈ
Sg Nom				
Sg Gen				
Sg Dat				
Sg Acc				
Pl Nom				
Pl Gen				
Pl Dat				
Pl Acc				

The visual cues are obvious, and these small but noticeable cues are conducive to learning and memorization. In this situation, every time students glance at this table (whether blank or completed) they are *visually* reminded that the singular dative ending is the same for all declesions and genders. Other examples could be given.

The vast majority of tables in this grammar bear this consideration in mind, and the result is that students have shapes and visual clues to work with as they memorize Greek instead of relying on "rote memory." In my teaching experience, these visually-sensitive modifications have proven to work well.

Some teachers will undoubtedly object to this approach, saying, "the old way is better because it requires students to know the material more *purely* without any help from visual arrangement; therefore they know the material *better*." But this simply isn't the case (no pun intended). The goal is not to have students learn Greek *grammar* according to text-based assertions, propositions, and rules, much less in their ability to fill in a blank page. What matters at the end of the day is that students can effectively *read Greek* by quickly and accurately implementing the knowledge they have obtained. In the end, what teaches better just teaches better.[31]

Fourth, this grammar is generally *concise*. What this means is that nothing is repeated unless necessary, and whatever is repeated is indicated as a repetition. One of the chief benefits of writing over oral discourse is that students can go back as many times as they want, on their own time, to review the material. This usually cannot happen when listening to a lecture. Literary educators often take advantage of this situation (as do publishers, who are concerned about manuscript length). But many do not simply because it is sometimes easier to learn things from literature if the literature is written like an oral conversation. People's default mode of thinking and interacting is typically orally-based,[32] so writing that reflects the tone, arrangement, and character of spoken conversation is more natural and therefore easy to absorb.

The trouble is that teaching a language—especially a "dead one" that often involves an acute degree of precision when it comes to biblical studies—simply cannot be taught in a textbook

---

[31] I am not suggesting that most grammarians would disagree with my assumption about visual clues. I personally believe the reason tables do not give attention to this matter is because the table modifications take so much time. (If the spread of this work were condensed into one chronological period, probably one of the eight years spent on producing this grammar was dedicated to improving visual cues and optimal presentation).

[32] Perhaps this embodies the larger fact that spoken langauages existed before written languages.

with the tone of spoken conversation. Now, I realize that some grammars attempt this as much as possible (e.g., Dobson). The idea is to teach the language in a way that is more "from the top down" (starting in conversation and readings) than the "bottom up" (starting in morphology and grammar). This text, like others, is a balance between these approaches because of the inherent advantages to it. But unlike the comparable lternatives, I avoid repetition unless necessary—especially in those cases where repetition is not clearly a repetitition. (I remember being frustrated in class during my college years when our textbook would summarize the chapter in different terms than in the beginning of the chapter, and I never knew if I was missing something. I quickly came to learn that *repeating things in different ways sometimes causes more confusion than clarity*). In many contexts, then, "less is more."

Fifth, I have tried to be fairly consistent when walking the fine line between "introductory" and "advanced." This is manifest in a number of ways that need not all be explained here. But it will suffice for the moment to note how this can vary with alternate methods. It is somewhat odd, for example, that Porter's volume includes a whole chapter on conditional sentences (which is a syntactical topic that doesn't strike one as "fundamental" for an introductory grammar). Mounce's "advanced information" at the end of certain chapters is also sometimes puzzling, since there doesn't always seem to be a clear reason why the material in each of these sections was included (e.g., additional types of genitive nouns are not, oddly, the most frequently used in NT Greek, when one would expect them to be). In short, there are many inconsistencies in today's grammars regarding the inclusion of "additional" material, and (as my classroom teaching can testify), this can really throw students for a loop.

Sixth, I kept in mind the transition that students will be going through from first year to second year Greek—something often overlooked by many grammars. Isolationist (or simply ignorant) approaches have unfortunately resulted in forceful unlearning or unnecessary re-learning when the time comes to go through second year Greek (which in recent times consists of Wallace's *Greek Grammar Beyond the Basics* or *The Basics of New Testament Syntax*). Other approaches attempt to address this challenge by simply making the first-year more advanced.

In my perspective, both of these approaches miss the mark. A grammar pedagogically disconnected from second-year publications and material (syntax and exegesis) causes unnecessary re-learning due to natural overlap in content, while a more advanced first-year grammar only puzzles students over the most basic material before even getting to syntax and exegesis. In contrast, this work has sought to reduce amount of the turbulence when transitioning to syntactical second-year work by modifying some of its structure, cross referencing key material, and using precise scholarly definitions instead of creating my own "temporary" (i. e. one-year) definitions. All of these improvements make the process of learning Greek easier and more efficient. Of course, if a student doesn't want a thorough knowledge of Greek, they won't be looking at a second year anyway. But in that case, I would argue that they probably shouldn't be taking the first year either! (See "a little bit of Greek is dangerous" below).

Seventh, related to the previous item mentoned above, I have intentionally and briefly exposed students to key grammatical debates and disagreements among grammatical definitions that other grammars typically ignore or obscure. So, for example, in the Grammatical Glosssary at the back of this book, I have included multiple definitions where grammarians generally disagree. The same goes for grammatical concepts, like the aspect of the future tense. This ensures that students not only resist the temptation to absolutize that which is relative, but to become aware of popular debates and discern the issues at stake.

Many grammarians object to this "error of absence" claim, saying something to the effect of, "first-year students don't need to know all about that; they should be spared such specialized discussions, so they should be left out." It is not always clear whether this constitutes a selfless concern instead a license to tyrannize one's own "modern" teaching. Whatever the case, my concern is simply that students are taught how to think critically instead of taking every word from their professor (or textbook) as the indisputable truth, because it often isn't. This is especially important in coursework that involve such specialized knowledge, which naturally gives teachers more indisputable authority. Students have every right to know when their professor or textbook is presenting material in a misleading fashion. Such misleading occurs often when substantial, alternative grammatical and definitional options are subtly absent or ignored.

Eighth, this grammar is different in that it is published with two companions, a workbook with both teacher and student versions. The vast majority of Greek textbooks do not have these tools—which is exactly why they do not become widely-used.

Even those that do have workbooks, they do not have teacher's editions. This is unfortunate, since the teacher's edition of the workbook contains not only accurate answers for the student edition (something lacking by even the most popular Greek workbooks[33]), but tests for classroom use as well. There are obviously a number of online tools for learning Greek, and some teachers may find them more beneficial than others. But in a prediably biased opinion, I think less work for the professor the better, so that's why I made the two-version workbook.[34]

Other noticeable differences include the workbook-requirement for reverse vocabulary entries, the utilization of multiple fonts, progressive exposure to table elements, and many others, each having utilizing a particular, pedagogical rationale. In the end, the book you hold is not simply a revision of any other published grammar, but is ultimately a hybrid of various approaches, works, and attitudes, designed to help students learn Greek as *efficiently* as possible. Only you can judge if it lives up to these goals. All mistakes are my own.

---

[33] In 2014, after going through Zondervan's *Basics of Biblical Syntax* text and workbook in class for second-year Greek, I documented over three solid pages of errors in conjunction with these two publications and Zondervan's complementary "answer sheet" for the workbook. (I submitted the error list to HarperOne and received a reply that my concerns are going to the right department; I guess this is better than nothing). Hopefully a revised edition of Wallace's text and workbook will eventually be published. Until then, I do not recommend that students use it for second-year Greek.

[34] For those that are concerned that students will purchase the teacher's edition and simply fill out the correct answers in the student edition, this is possible (as it is with countless other College courses, many texts having answers in the back of the student's book), though the student will certainly fail the course this way since they would not be able to past the tests.

Preface to the First Edition

How to Use This Grammar

In addition to preparing students for second year Greek, both the *Concise Greek Grammar* textbook and workbook are designed to be completed within two regular academic semesters at either a college or graduate level. In addition to the workbook and grammar, students should also purchase a number of other essential resources. Below is a *suggested* curriculum for the first three years:

First Year Greek
Jamin Andreas Hübner, *A Concise Greek Grammar*
Jamin Andreas Hübner, *A Concise Greek Grammar Workbook*
Barclay Newman and Florian Voss, eds., *The UBS Greek New Testament: Reader's Edition with Textual Notes* (2015), 5th Edition
Frederick Danker, *The Concise Greek-English Lexicon of the New Testament* (2009)
Philip Comfort, *A Commentary on the Manuscripts and Text of the New Testament* (2015)
Greek flashcards (physical or digital)
Bible translations (hard copy or digital online): NRSV, NIV, CEB

Recommended Summer Reading
Mark Powell, *Introduction to the New Testament* (2018)
Joel Green and Martin McDonald, eds., *The World of the New Testament* (2013)
D. A. Carson, *Exegetical Fallacies* (1996)

Second Year Greek (*Academic Track*)
Daniel Wallace, *Greek Grammar Beyond the Basics* (1998)
Philip Comfort, *New Testament Text and Translation Commentary* (2008)
The Greek-English New Testament (2015)
John Hayes and Carl Holladay, *Biblical Exegesis* (2007)
Supplemental/Optional Material for Case Studies: Michael Holmes, ed., *The Apostolic Fathers* (2007) Jamin Hübner, "Revisiting αὐθεντέω in 1 Timothy 2:12," *The Journal for the Study of Paul and His Letters* 5:1 (2015). *Lexham's Syntactical Greek New Testament* (digital only)

Second Year Greek (*Pastoral Track*)
Philip Comfort, *New Testament Text and Translation Commentary* (2008)
The Greek-English New Testament (2015)
Gordon Fee, *New Testament Exegesis* (2002)
Wright, *The New Testament For Everyone* commentary series (2011)

Recommended Summer Reading
Moisés Silva and Karen Jobes, *An Invitation to the Septuagint* (2015)
Timothy Law, *When God Spoke Greek* (2013)

Third Year Greek
Alfred Ralphs and Robert Hanhart, eds., *Septuaginta* (2007)
Albert Pietersma and Benjamin Wright, *A New English Translation of the Septuagint* (2007)
Takamitsu Muraoka, *A Greek-English Lexicon of the Septuagint* (2010)
Takamitsu Muraoka, *A Greek-Hebrew/Aramaic Two-way Index to the Septuagint* (2010)

I always require students to have their Greek New Testament with them (*UBS5 Reader's Edition with Textual Notes*), regardless of what year of study they are in. Note also that the resources build from one year to the next; the resources listed under year two are *in addition* to those listed in year one. The same is true for year two and three.

1 Alphabet, Pronunciation, and Punctuation

1.1 Alphabet

Name	Capital	Small	Examples	Name in Greek
Alpha	A	α	Alm or apple	ἄλφα
Beta	B	β	Victory	βῆτα
Gamma	Γ	γ	yellow/goat	γάμμα
Delta	Δ	δ	those	δέλτα
Epsilon	E	ε	Energy	ἔψιλόν
Zeta	Z	ζ	Zebra/suds	ζῆτα
Eta	H	η	Café	ἦτα
Theta	Θ	θ	Thumb	θῆτα
Iota	I	ι	Fin/Ski	ἰῶτα
Kappa	K	κ	Kids	κάππα
Lambda	Λ	λ	Link	λάμβδα
Mu	M	μ	Monkey	μῦ
Nu	N	ν	Name	νῦ
Xi	Ξ	ξ	Axiom	ξῖ
Omicron	O	ο	Open	ὄμικρόν
Pi	Π	π	Popcorn	πῖ
Rho	P	ρ	Rule	ῥῶ
Sigma	Σ	σ/ς	Student	σίγμα
Tau	T	τ	Tutor	ταῦ
Upsilon	Y	υ	Skew (über)	ὐψιλόν
Phi	Φ	φ	Photon	φῖ
Chi	X	χ	Loch	χῖ
Psi	Ψ	ψ	Tips	ψῖ
Omega	Ω	ω	Cone	ὠμέγα

Chapter One: Alphabet, Pronunciation, and Punctuation

1.1.1 Koiné Greek is a snapshot of the Greek language in time, with ancient/classical Greek overlapping before it and Byzantine Greek overlapping after it.[1] For the same reason, the Koiné Greek alphabet has blurred edges—especially when it comes to numbers. Here are two examples:

1.1.1.1 The digamma or wau (ϝ) is an older letter that came after epsilon in the alphabet and had a "w" sound. It sometimes appears when studying verbal morphology and can function as the numeral 6 and 16.

1.1.1.2 Another example is the stigma (a ligature combining σ and τ) or vau (ϛ), "an old letter infrequently appearing in later Greek [also] used as the numeral *six*" (e.g. Rev 13:18) and 16.[2]

1.1.2 Basic numerals, other than their Roman form (I, II, II, IV, etc.), can be expressed in letters by adding an acute accent after them. For example, α´ is 1 and β´ is 2. Iotas added before the sign adds 1. So, ιβ´ is 12. For thousands, restart at α and use a lower stroke preceding the letter. So ͵β is 2,000, and ͵βα is 2,001. Below is a table of the most common numerals in the New Testament in their various written expressions.[3]

#	Sign	Cardinal	Ordinal	Adverbial
1	α´	εἷς, μία, ἕν, *one*	πρῶτος, -η, -ον, *first*	ἅπαξ, *once*
2	β´	δύο, *two*	δεύτερος, -α, -ον, *second*	δίς, *twice*
3	γ´	τρεῖς, τρία, *three*	τρίτος, -η, -ον, *third*	τρεῖς, *thrice*
7	ζ´	ἑπτά, *seven*	ἕβδομος, η, -ον, *seventh*	ἑπτάκις, *seven times*
10	ι´	δέκα, *ten*	δέκατος, -η, -ον, *ten*	δεκάκις, *ten times*
12	ιβ´	δώδεκα, *twelve*	δωδέκατος, -η, -ον, *twelfth*	δωδεκάκις, *twelve times*
100	ρ´	ἑκατόν, *hundred*	ἑκατοστός, -ή, -όν, *hundredth*	ἑκατοντάκις, *a hundred times*
1000	͵α	χίλιοι, -αι, -α, *thousand*	χιλιοιστός, -ή, -όν, *thousandth*	χιλιάκις, *a thousand times*

---

[1] "Modern Greek" comes even later.
[2] *CL*, 159. Cf. Porter, *Fundamentals,* 361. Porter also notes koppa (ϙ) for 90 and sampi (ϡ) for 900.
[3] It is not necessary to memorize all of these forms now. You will learn the most common ones in later chapters.

1.1.3 When writing Greek letters, most small and capital letters go above the line.[4] However, as you may have already noticed, β, γ, ζ, ξ, μ, ρ, χ, and ψ extend below the line.

1.1.4 All Greek letters can be written in one or two strokes. The exception is π, which must be written in three strokes.

1.1.5 Greek letters may appear different depending on the font or style of writing.[5]

1.1.5.1 ϑ (one stroke) = θ (two stroke)

1.1.5.2 ϰ (one-stroke) = κ (two-stroke)

1.1.5.3 ϱ (one stroke) = ρ (one stroke)

1.1.5.4 ϕ (one stroke) = φ (two stroke)

1.1.6 Sigmas in Greek are written in two ways: *medial sigmas* (σ) for the beginning or middle of a word, and *final sigmas* (ς) for the end of a word. Example: ἀπόστολος.

1.2 Pronunciation of Consonants

1.2.1 Greek pronunciation varies according to the type of Greek (e.g., Ancient, Koiné, Byzantine, Modern), dialect (e.g., Aeolic, Doric, Ionic, Mycenaean, Attic), and pronunciation system (e.g., Attic, Erasmian, "restored" Koiné, Modern). Most academics today use the (Americanized) Erasmian system because it is similar to English and therefore easy to learn.[6] However, for the sake of being more accurate, this grammar will follow the "restored" Koiné pronunciation used for Koiné Greek.[7]

---

[4] The distinction between uppercase ("uncial") and lowercase ("miniscule") Greek letters generally emerged in the 800s AD.
[5] The one-stroke variants are today often referred to as "cursive" or "longhand."
[6] The major differences between Erasmian and Koiné pronunciation is that in Erasmian, (1) diphthongs αι, ει, and οι directly correspond to the English diphthongs ai, ei, and oi; (2) ω and o are pronounced long and short; (3) β, δ, γ are soft fricatives while φ, θ, χ are hard fricatives (instead of the reverse—as noted in this section).
[7] Cf. Decker, *Reading*, 11-16.

Chapter One: Alphabet, Pronunciation, and Punctuation

1.2.2   There are three basic consonantal sounds:

1.2.2.1 *Labial* — These are sounds made with the lips, such as the letters π, φ, and β. Say "pie," "phone," and "voice."

1.2.2.2 *Velar* — These are sounds made with the tongue, which blocks and releases airflow by moving up and down. They include κ, χ, and γ. Say "cowboy," "loch," and "yesterday."

1.2.2.3 *Dental* — These are sounds made with the teeth and tongue; the tongue touches the teeth to block and release airflow. They include τ, θ, and δ. Say "tea," "thankyou," "these."

1.2.3   Sounds that completely stop airflow are called *stops*. The Greek stops are π, κ, and τ.

1.2.4   Sounds that slow airflow by friction are called *fricatives*. Fricatives that generate a lot of friction are "hard" fricatives (φ, χ, θ),[8] and fricatives that generate little friction are "soft" fricatives (β, γ, δ).

1.2.5   Each of these consonantal sounds may combine with a sigma to contract into another Greek consonant. While this may change the letters, it does not change the pronunciation:

1.2.5.1 When a σ is added to a Labial letter, the two form a ψ.

1.2.5.2 When a σ is added to a Velar letter, the two form a ξ.

1.2.5.3 When a σ is added to a Dental letter, the two condense into a σ.

Example: οπ + σομαι = οψομαι
Example: σαρκ + σι = σαρξι.

1.2.6   These contractions, along with all of the stops and fricatives, can be summarized in the *Table of Stops and Fricatives*.[9]

---

[8] Hard fricatives also tend to produce a lot of spitting!
[9] If each row is pronounced outloud, readers will notice how air resistance decreases and airflow increases when moving from the left to the right side of the table.

	Stops	**Fricatives**		
		Hard	*Soft*	
Labial	π	φ	β	ψ
Velar	κ	χ	γ	ξ
Dental	τ	θ	δ	σ

1.2.7   Additional rules of pronouncing consonants:

1.2.7.1   Gammas are softly pronounced like a "y" sound ("young") when followed by an ε, ι, or η. Otherwise, they are pronounced hard like a "g" sound ("grass").

1.2.7.2   When a gamma is followed by any velar letter (κ, χ, γ or ξ), it is pronounced with an "n" sound. Example: the first γ in εὐαγγέλιον (gospel) is pronounced like an "n," so the whole word sounds like "*evanyellion.*" This is called a *gamma nasal*.

1.2.7.3   Zetas are pronounced like the English z ("zoo") when it is the first letter of a word (e.g., ζωή). In all other cases (e.g., βαπτίζω), it is pronounced with a "dz" sound ("suds").

1.3   Pronunciation of Vowels and Diphthongs

1.3.1   The seven Greek vowels are α, ε, η, ι, ο, υ, and ω.

1.3.2   Alpha (α) and iota (ι) are pronounced either long or short.

    Short: "rather" and "pin," like βαπτίζω and ἵνα

    Long: "father" and "pizza," like ἀμήν and περί

1.3.3   Iotas at the beginning of a word have a "y" sound. Example: Ἰησοῦς (Jesus or Joshua) is pronounced "*yay-soos.*"

1.3.4   Upsilon (υ) is pronounced as a "high rounded" vowel (ü).[10] This is difficult for English speakers since there is no direct equivalent. The sound is made by saying a long ē sound (like "eat" or "feet") and then rounding the lips in a circle shape. (It

---

[10] It is called "high-rounded" because the tongue is high and the lips are rounded when pronounced. Examples: über, Jamin Hübner, Kürt Aland. German speakers will not have trouble here since it is a regular part of the language.

Chapter One: Alphabet, Pronunciation, and Punctuation

might help to think of it as a half-way point between *ēē* and *ōō*.)[11] Example: κύριος. The closest English comes to this sound is in words ending in "ew" like "sk<u>ew</u>" and "d<u>ew</u>." But even this is not a direct equivalent because both vowels are pronounced in two combined sounds instead of one sound.

1.3.5 ε and α often lengthen to η, and ο often lengthens to ω at the end of words (largely because of similar pronunciation).

Example: the verb λύο = λύω

Example: the noun θεοι = θεῳ

1.3.6 A pair of vowels can be pronounced separately.

Example: the name Ἀβρα<u>ά</u>μ (ah-br<u>ah</u>-<u>ah</u>m)

1.3.7 A pair of vowels that produce a single sound is called a *diphthong*. Greek diphthongs can be summarized the following *Table of Greek Diphthongs*.

Diphthong	Eng. Examples	Greek Examples
αι	B<u>e</u>t	κ<u>αι</u> (and, even, but)
ει	Rec<u>ei</u>ve	<u>εἰ</u>πον (he/she said)
οι	<u>Ü</u>ber	<u>οἰ</u>κία (house, home)
υι	S<u>ui</u>te	<u>υἱ</u>ός (son)
αυ	<u>Af</u>ter/<u>av</u>enue	<u>αὐ</u>τός (he, she, it)
ου	Gr<u>ou</u>p	<u>ὂυ</u>τος (this, these)
ευ, ηυ	Eff<u>e</u>ct/<u>e</u>very	πορ<u>εύ</u>ομαι (I go, live)

1.3.8 The second vowel of a Greek dipthong is always an ι or an υ.

1.3.9 Αυ is pronounced like the hard fricative "<u>af</u>ter" when used before a stop (κ, π, τ) or before a hard fricative (φ, χ, θ). In all other cases, it is pronounced like the soft fricative "<u>av</u>enue."

---

[11] Many English-speakers sometimes say the word "dude" this way (neither "dood" nor "deed," but "düde").

1.3.10 Ευ and ηυ are pronounced like the hard fricative "e<u>ff</u>ect" when used before a stop (π, κ, τ) or before a hard fricative (φ, χ, θ). In all other cases, it is pronounced like the soft fricative "e<u>v</u>ent."

1.3.11 An *improper diphthong* is made up of an α, η, or ω and an *iota subscript* (a small iota under a vowel). It is not pronounced. Example: ὥρᾳ (hour, occasion, moment) is pronounced "hor<u>ah</u>," not "hor<u>eh</u>."

1.3.12 Sometimes diphthongs are not pronounced at all. In these rare cases, a *dieresis* (two dots) is placed over the second vowel to show that both vowels are pronounced separately. Example: Ἠσαΐας (Isaiah), or the English word "naïve" ("*nah-eeve*," not "*nev*" or "*nave*").[12]

1.4 Accents

1.4.1 *Accents* primarily indicate where stress is placed in the pronunciation of a word.

1.4.2 English words do not contain accents. Example: the word "coupon" has stress over the letters o and u (first syllable), but in the word "up<u>o</u>n" the stress is over the letter o (second syllable). There is no accent to indicate this change in pronunciation; speakers simply have to remember it.

1.4.3 Languages like Greek (and Spanish, French, etc.), however, regularly use a variety accents.[13] Example: the Spanish words "música" and "panadería," and the Greek words αἰτέω (I ask) and λόγος (word).

1.4.4 Accents also distinguish two different words that are otherwise spelled the same.

1.4.4.1 Since English words normally do not contain accents, students have to catch on and learn what the different meanings of the same word are. Example: the word "bow" can be a verb that

---

[12] The vast majority of NT and LXX words with a dieresis come from Greek names transliterated from Hebrew or Aramaic.

[13] Hence, Greek is "polytonic" ("many-toned").

Chapter One: Alphabet, Pronunciation, and Punctuation

means to stoop over, or "bow" can be a noun that's a hunting device that shoots arrows. Context determines which is used.

1.4.4.2 Languages like Greek, however, use accents regularly to differentiate between two different meanings. Example: the Spanish word "papa" means "potato," but "papá" means "father." Likewise, the Greek word τίς means "who?" but τις means a certain "someone" or "something." Another example is ἣν ("which") and ἦν ("was").

1.4.5 Accents appear in one of three places in a word:

1.4.5.1 Last syllable (*ultima*). Example: οὐραν_ό_ν

1.4.5.2 Second from last syllable (*penult*). Example: προφῆτης

1.4.5.3 Third from last syllable (*antepenult*). Example: ἀπ_ό_στολος

1.4.6 Greek accents have three different variations:

1.4.6.1 *Acute*: ό (pronounced with a high and rising pitch)

1.4.6.2 *Grave*: ὸ (pronounced with a low and falling pitch)

1.4.6.3 *Circumflex*: ῶ or ῶ.[14] (no change in pronunciation)

1.4.7 Grave accents only fall on an ultima, while circumflex accents only fall on an ultima or penult.

1.4.8 Unaccented syllables are considered to have grave accents even if they aren't visible.

1.4.9 Accents change their variation according to their positions in words and in sentences.

1.4.9.1 To compensate for change in pronunciation, acute accents often move in a word that has gained or lost letters.

Example: ἄγγελος ("angel") → ἀγγ_έ_λοις ("angels")[15]

1.4.9.2 Grave accents change to acute accents if they are not followed by another Greek word.

---

[14] The difference between a curve and tiddle is a matter of font and personal preference.
[15] Cf. English (accents added to indicate stress), "rátify" to "ratificátion."

Example: ἐστὶν ἡ βασιλεία → ἐστίν
→ ἐστίν the kingdom
→ "ἐστίν."

1.4.10 Circumflexes are added over vowel contractions.[16]

Example: λογο + ο = λογοῦ

1.4.11 When an accent recedes as far as possible from the end of a word to the beginning (to the antepenult or whatever syllable is first), the word is *recessive*. This occurs with finite verbs.

1.4.12 When a word that normally doesn't have an accent takes one from the previous word, this word is *enclitic*.[17] This occurs frequently with first and second personal pronouns (like μου, μοι, σου, σοι, etc.), indefinite pronouns (like τις) and some adverbs and particles (like οὐ, πως, and others)

1.4.13 When a word otherwise retains the accent instead of moving around like all of these cases, it is *retentive*.

1.5 Breathing Marks

1.5.1 Greek words beginning with vowels or rho (ρ) always have one of two types of *breathing marks*:

1.5.1.1 Smooth breathing mark: These breathing marks look like a normal apostrophe and are placed over the first vowel. They do not affect pronunciation. Example: ἰδού (behold) is pronounced just like it appears: "ithoo."

1.5.1.2 Rough breaking mark: These breathing marks look like a backwards apostrophe and are placed over the first vowel of a word to create an "h" sound. Example: ὅτι (that, since, because) is pronounced like "hotee."

---

[16] See chapter 8 for the rules of contraction.
[17] Note: An enclitic takes its own accent when it stands at the beginning of a sentence (since it isn't preceded by a word). A *proclitic* is a word that does not take its own accent, unless it precedes an enclitic (e.g., ὁ, ἡ, οἱ, αἱ, εἰς, ἐκ, etc.).

1.5.2   A rho (ρ) at the beginning of a word always has a rough breathing mark, never a smooth.

1.5.3   For words that begin with a diphthong, a breathing mark is placed over the second vowel. Example: αἰτέω (I ask, demand)

1.5.4   For words that begin with two vowels that don't form a diphthong, the breathing mark is placed in front of the capital letter. Example: Ἰησοῦς.

1.6 Punctuation

1.6.1   Commas and periods function the same way in Greek as they do in English. But, semicolons and question marks function differently.

1.6.1.1 The English semicolon functions the same as the Greek question mark. Example: Ἰησοῦ Χριστοῦ; = "Jesus Christ?"

1.6.1.2 A *mid-dot* functions the same as the English colon or semicolon. Example: Ἰησοῦ Χριστοῦ· = "Jesus Christ;" or "Jesus Christ:"

1.6.2   Greek does not distinguish between a colon and a semicolon in its use of mid-dots. (Since the meaning of the two is very different, it is important to be aware of this when interpreting passages with mid-dots.) Translations will sometimes render the conjunction "for" (γάρ) by using a colon.[18]

1.6.3   Greek has no quotation mark, so discerning the presence, start, or ending of a quote can be challenging. However, many published Greek New Testament editions (e.g., *UBS*) indicate quotations by capitalizing the first letter of a quote. This makes identifying quotations easy.[19] Example:

---

[18] E.g., Gal 4:24 (ESV and NASB).
[19] However, it is important to remember that the addition of capital letters at the beginning of quotes are modern editorial additions; the first-century New Testament was written without punctuation and in all capital letters, so it is sometimes debated what was, in fact, originally intended to be a quotation.

μὴ οὖν μεριμνήσητε λέγοντες, Τί φάγωμεν; ἤ, Τί πίωμεν;
So do not worry saying, "<u>W</u>hat will we eat?" or, "<u>W</u>hat will we drink?"[20]

1.6.4 Like English, the first letter of a paragraph (though not necessarily every sentence) is capitalized.

1.7 **Tips on Studying**

1.7.1 As with learning any new language, students should say everything out loud when writing or reading Greek. The more sources of exposure to the language (sight, sound, etc.), the better. Simply reading vocabulary to one's self is not adequate.

1.7.2 One of the best ways to initially learn the Greek alphabet is to transliterate English words into Greek letters. For example, make up a phrase like "It is tuesday," and then write it out as best as possible in Greek letters: "Ιτ ισ τυεζδη." Or, "Cats are smart" = "κατς αρε σμαρτ."

1.7.3 Like all languages, Greek is flexible. This is because languages are human phenomena, and human beings aren't computers.[21] Do not be surprised when rules have exceptions and lines have fuzzy edges.

1.8 **Vocabulary**

1.8.1 Vocabulary is crucial to learn. It is more important than grammar because grammatical rules are only as good as the words that follow those rules. Below is a typical list of vocabulary words:

---

[20] Mt 6:31.
[21] It is unfortunate that anyone must say this, but since modernity the metaphors of people being "machines," having brains that are "computers," are no longer being recognized as the metaphors that they are. See Wendell Berry, *The Miracle of Life: An Essay Against Modern Superstition* (Washington D.C.: Counterpoint, 2001) and David Bently Hart, *Atheist Delusions* (New Haven: Yale University Press, 2009).

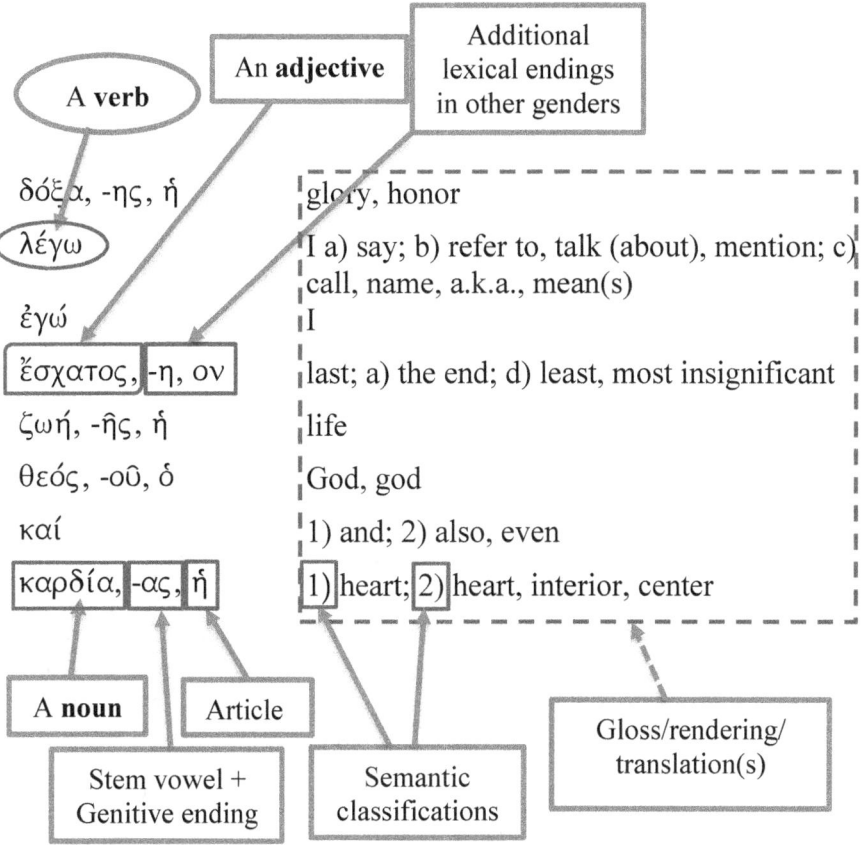

1.8.2 As you can see, a typical noun vocab entry consists of three things: the noun (in its *lexical form*), the stem vowel and singular genitive case ending, and the singular article in one of three genders (ὁ, ἡ, τό).

1.8.2.1 The "lexical form" (or *lemma*) of a word is the form of a word as it appears in a lexicon (or dictionary). So for example, the lexical form of the English word "singing" is "sing." Although the word "sing" can have a number of different forms (sing, singing, sang, sung, singingly, etc.), only one is fully defined in a dictionary: sing (which is singular in number and in present tense). Greek works in a similar way.

1.8.2.2 The lexical form of Greek nouns and adjectives is always (unless noted) in the *nominative* case and is *singular* in number.[22]

1.8.2.3 The lexical form of Greek verbs are always (unless noted) written in the *present* tense-stem, *first* person, and *indicative* mood.

1.8.3 These aspects will be explained more thoroughly in the next chapter. For now, just know that the vocabulary list must be memorized, and that this is regular part of learning the language.

1.8.3.1 15 minutes a day is often sufficient for the average student. Flashcards (whether physical or digital) are a proven method of effectively learning new vocabulary, and are therefore recommended.

1.8.3.2 When definitions of vocabulary are excessively long, it is only necessary to memorize the *first two renderings of each semantic category*. For example, the vocabulary entry for καρδία, –ας, ἡ is "1) heart; 2) heart, interior, center." You must memorize the whole entry except for "center." (Depending on your teacher, extra credit may be obtained by completing the *entire* vocabulary entry on tests and the workbook.)[23]

1.8.3.3 For prepositions, the case each rendering functions with must be memorized. For example, the preposition διά has the following entry: "a) w. gen. through; b) w. acc. through, because of." This means that διά should be rendered "through" when modifying a genitive word, or "through" or "because of"

---

[22] Compare with English dictionaries (e.g., when coming across the plural form of "cars," the dictionary won't define it, but will instead say "see 'car'").

[23] In cases where *CL* provides renderings *prior* to semantic categorizations, only the initial renderings need to be memorized. For example, in the entry "ἐγείρω rise, raise; a) get up; b) awaken, rouse, raise, rise; c) rise, appear, go," only the first two glosses "rise, raise" need to be memorized.
In cases where prepositions function with different cases are embedded within semantic categories, the first two renderings of each case must be memorized. For example, the third semantic category of παρά is "3) w. acc. alongside, near; dat: beside, in the presence of; acc: alongside of." All of this must be memorized.

when modifying an accusative word. Both the rendering and the case of the word it modifies must be memorized.

1.8.4 The vocabulary definitions used in this grammar follow both the renderings and semantic categories presented in Danker's *Concise Greek-English Lexicon.* This is both for convenience (assuming students are using this lexicon as they study this grammar) and for long-term growth (transitioning into the full, scholarly lexicon of most English-speaking academic communities, *BDAG*, is virtually effortless).

1.8.5 However, vocabulary lists in this grammar are not simply cut and paste from the *Concise Lexicon,* because it is impossible (an unnecessary) for students to memorize all the lexical information for each word (especially in the first year of Greek). So there are a few rules I followed to aid summarization:

1.8.5.1 Only major glosses/translations[24] (those that *CL* makes **bold italic**) are included. Occasionally, I add a gloss for the sake of popularity (e.g., adding "(trad. 'Amen') to the entry of ἀμήν, or adding "2) accompany" to the entry of ἀκολουθέω).

1.8.5.2 Renderings are repeated only if they appear in more than one semantic category. This is to avoid unnecessary repetition without collapsing the different senses. Example:

ὁδός, -οῦ, ἡ   1) <u>way</u>, road, highway, path; 2) <u>way</u>, journey, trip, the Way

1.8.5.3 Categories are also consolidated if they share the same rendering. This is to avoid unnecessary repetition without falsely suggesting that there is only one sense.

Example: εἰρήνη, -ης, ἡ   1-2) peace

---

[24] Some contend that a "gloss" and "translation" are not exactly the same. A gloss, as used in Greek lexicons, is an English-word generally representing the closest "meaning" or "meanings" of the Greek term (a "context-free" rendering). A translation is the same—except that it refers to a specific textual context (a "contextually-sensitive" gloss). However, this is not, in fact, how many grammarians use the two terms; a "gloss" can also be the final inflected form/rendering of a word in a specific context. For that reason, it is not important to distinguish sharply between the two.

1.8.5.4 Categories are not included if it cannot be characterized by a major gloss/translation. (For this reason, you may notice skipping of numbers, such as a jump from semantic category 2 to 4.)

1.8.5.5 The following graphic is a sample vocabulary entry from *Concise Lexicon*.

ἄξιος, α, ον [cp. ἄγω in sense of 'draw down' in the scale = 'weigh'; s. ἀναξίως]—1. 'having worth or value', **worthy,**—ἀξία πρός of no importance relative to Ro 8:18.—2. 'in accordance with expectation of worth', **appropriate**, *fitting, compatible*—Mt 3:8; Lk 3:8; 23:41; Ac 26:20; 2 Th 1:3. Impers. ἄξιόν ἐστι *it is appropriate* 1 Cor 16:4. —3. 'possessing merit or value that deserves praise', **worthy, meriting,** *deserving*—a. in a positive sense, of one who merits recommendation/commendation, with thing merited as reward, with gen. or inf., and sometimes with negation: Mt 10:10; Lk 10:7 = 1 Ti 5:18; Lk 15:19, 21; Ac 13:46; 1 Ti 6:1; Hb 11:38; Rv 4:11 al. Abs. Mt 10:11, 13; 22:8; Rv 3:4. Other syntactical formulations: Lk 7:4; Ac 13:25 (cp. J 1:27). In Mt 10:37f the point is that those who give preferential treatment to relatives at the expense of honoring Jesus in effect dishonor themselves.—b. pejoratively, of actions or conditions deserving/meriting appropriate penalty: blows Lk 12:48; most freq. death 23:15 al. Of pers. meriting penalty Ro 1:32; abs., but in ref. to the narrative that precedes, Rv 16:6.

1. Headword
2. Etymology or derivation in brackets
3. Arabic numeral introducing major semantic classification
4. Extended definition in single quotes
5. Brief rendering or gloss in bold italics
6. Lightface gloss as suggestion for rendering Greek in a specific passage
7. Biblical references
8. Letter introducing subset of major classification
9. Additional nuancing or further detail followed by pertinent biblical references

Vocabulary

Ἀβραάμ, ὁ	Abraham
ἄγγελος, -ου, ὁ	messenger, envoy, attendant (trad. *angel*)
ἀμήν	amen (so let it be)
ἄνθρωπος, -ου, ὁ	a human being, person, someone, somebody
ἀπόστολος, -ου, ὁ	a) messenger, delegate; b) ambassador, apostle, envoy
Γαλιλαία, -ας, ἡ	Galilee
γραφή, -ῆς, ἡ	scripture
Δαυίδ, ὁ	David
δόξα, -ης, ἡ	glory, honor
ἐγώ	I
ἔσχατος, -η, -ον	last; a) the end; d) least, most insignificant
ζωή, -ῆς, ἡ	life
θεός, -οῦ, ὁ	God, god
καί	1) and; 2) also, even
καρδία, -ας, ἡ	1) heart; 2) heart, interior, center
κόσμος, -ου, ὁ	1) adornment; 2) universe, world; 3-4) world
λόγος, -ου, ὁ	1) word, statement, message, speech; 2) word, reason
Παῦλος, -ου, ὁ	Paul
Πέτρος, -ου, ὁ	Peter
Πιλᾶτος, -ου, ὁ	Pilate
πνεῦμα, -ατος, τό	1) wind, breath, spirit; 3) spirit, apparition, ghost; 4) spirit, holy spirit
προφήτης, -ου, ὁ	1-2) prophet
σάββατον, -ου, τό	1) Sabbath; 2) week
Σίμων, -ωνος, ὁ	Simon
φωνή, -ῆς, ἡ	1) sound, noise; 2) voice, tone; 3) language
Χριστός, -οῦ, ὁ	1) the Anointed one, Messiah, Christ; 2) Christ

2 First and Second Declension Nouns

2.1 General Morphology

2.1.1 The smallest grammatical unit of language is a *morpheme*. *Morphology* is the study of morphemes.

2.1.2 A morpheme may be freestanding ("independent"), or it may be bound ("dependent") to other morphemes.

2.1.2.1 A morpheme that is "free" or "independent" is called a *root*. Roots are the most basic forms of words. They "convey distinctive content" or "carry the most significant meaning," and they cannot be further analyzed or broken down. A noun, adjective, or verb may or may not share the same root. For example, in English, the verb "be<u>friend</u>" and the adjective "<u>friend</u>ly" share the same root "friend." In Greek, the noun γραφή (writing) shares the same root as the verb γράφω (I write).[1]

2.1.2.2 A morpheme that is "bound" or "dependent" is an *affix*. Bound morphemes at the beginning of a word are *prefixes*, while bound morphemes at the end of a word are *suffixes*. To use the same example from above, the adjective "friendly" has the suffix "ly" to indicate that it describing an attribute.

2.1.3 A *stem* is the most basic form of a *particular kind* of root, like a noun, adjective, or verb. Stems often undergo some kind of change. You will not see them stand alone in a sentence because they combine with other morphemes to perform different grammatical functions. For example, the stem of the word

---

[1] Compound words, like "wheelchair" and "housesit," contain two roots.

"friendships" is "friendship," while the root is "friend." (The two suffixes are "ship" and "s.")

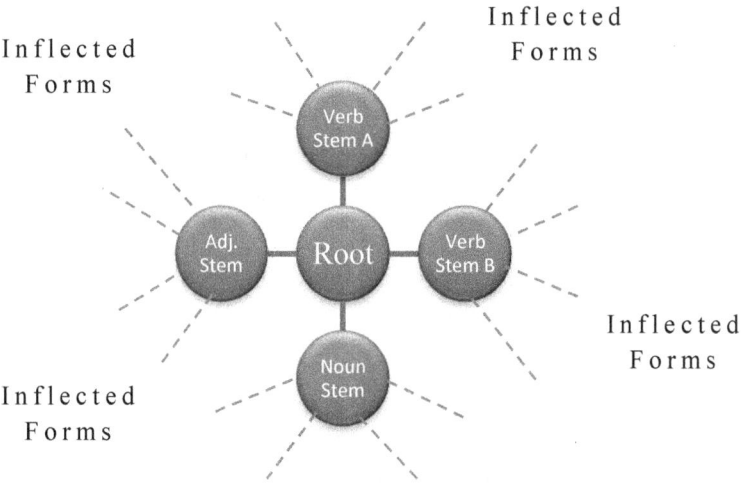

2.1.4   *Inflection* is when a word changes form according to the rules of grammar. To use the same example above, "friendship" *inflected* to "friendships" in order to exhibit plurality.

2.1.4.1   Inflection of nouns is called *declension*. When a noun changes into a particular form, it *declines*.

2.1.4.2   A noun that cannot decline is *indeclinable*. Example: Βεελζεβούλ (Beelezebul) and Ἰεσσαί (Jesse) never change.

2.1.4.3   Inflection of verbs is called *conjugation*. When a verb changes into a particular form, it *conjugates*. A verb that cannot conjugate is *inconjugatable*.

2.1.4.4   The inflected form of a word (as in parsing) is also called a *gloss* (though a "gloss" might refer to a specific translation, or general definition).

2.1.5   One can see, then, that a single root may have many stems, and these stems can combine with many morphemes to form even more inflected forms. Words can be used in countless ways!

2.1.6   To make things easier (more complicated), morphologists, lexicographers, and linguists have tried to simplify matters by (abstractly) combining all the various forms of words into groups headed by a single word called a *headword* or *lexeme*.

2.1.6.1   It is legitimate to say that a list of headwords with definitions is a *dictionary* and a list of lexemes with definitions is a *lexicon*. However, there is generally no difference between the two.[2]

2.1.7   Common lexemes used in popular and accepted lexicons/dictionaries are called *lemma* ("citation form").

2.1.8   Thus, the "lexical form" of a word is the form that appears in a lexicon, and a "lemma" is almost always the exact same as the "lexical form."[3]

2.2   The Morphology of Greek Nouns

2.2.1   A *noun* is the name of something (such as a person, animal, place, thing, quality, idea, or action) and is typically used in a sentence as subject, or object of a verb, or as object of a preposition. (See examples of this below)

2.2.2   A *substantive* is any word or group of words that function as a noun. Thus, a substantive may be a noun, pronoun, phrase, clause, etc. In the English examples below, the substantive is underlined:

Example: <u>The singing</u> made my ears hurt. (participle)
Example: <u>She</u> washed the car before supper. (personal pronoun)
Example: <u>"Once upon a time"</u> appears at the beginning of many children's stories. (phrase)

The suffixes of Greek nouns are called *case endings*. As such, case endings determine the way a noun functions in a clause.

---

[2] Lexicons sometimes tend to be more narrow and technical (focusing on words), while dictionaries often have a broader scope (focusing on phrases, concepts, etc.).
[3] Cf. 1.8.2.

$$\lambda o \gamma^*$$

(root)

$$\lambda o \gamma o$$

(noun stem)
(root + stem vowel)

$$\lambda o \gamma o \varsigma$$

(noun stem + case ending)

2.2.3   As noted above, when the stem and case ending of a noun combine to form the word as it exists in a sentence, it "inflects" or "declines." So, to exhibit plurality to "friend," an "s" is added. To exhibit ownership, I add an apostrophe and then an s ("friend's").

2.2.4   Greek works in a similar manner, although words are much more inflected; they can accomplish much more.

2.2.5   Case endings reflect four cases[4] for four general purposes:

2.2.5.1   *Nominative Case* — noun functions as the **subject** (which performs, receives, or experiences the action of the sentence).

2.2.5.2   *Genitive Case* — noun **modifies** another noun (the "head noun") to indicate a relationship (e.g., possession, inclusion, exclusion, origination, description, attribution, etc.). Genitives usually use the keywords "of," "from," or "by" in translation.

---

[4] There is a fifth ending called the *vocative case*, the "case of direct address," (e.g., Mt 7:21), but it is very rare. The three grammatical rules for the vocative are: 1) In the plural, the vocative is the same as the nominative plural; 2) in the singular first declension, the vocative is the same as the nominative; 3) In the singular second declension, the vocative ending is usually ε.

2.2.5.3   *Dative Case* — noun functions as the **indirect object** (which indirectly receives the action of the subject). Uses the keywords "to," "in," or "with" in translation.

2.2.5.4   *Accusative Case* — noun functions as the **direct object** (which directly receives the action of the subject).

2.2.6   To undertand how this case system works, it may be helpful to review how it works in comparison to the English language.[5] Observe the examples below:

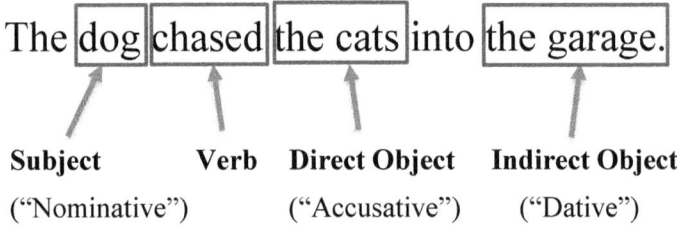

Subject   **Verb**   **Direct Object**   **Indirect Object**
("Nominative")   ("Accusative")   ("Dative")

2.2.7   If this sentence were in Greek, "the dog" would have a nominative singular case ending since one dog (singular) is performing the verb of the sentence. "The cat" would have an accusative plural case ending since they (plural) are receiving the action of the subject. Finally, "the garage" would be in the dative singular case, since it indirectly receives the action of the subject.[6] There is no genitive word in this example. So let's do another example with the genitive:

---

[5] In case you may be wondering, English has three cases: *subjective*, *objective*, *possessive*, loosely corresponding to the nominative, accusative, and genitive respectively.

[6] Indirect objects also often function as the "object of the preposition" because they come before a preposition (e.g., "to," "in," "with," etc.), as in this example ("into the garage"). But, sometimes no preposition is used. Compare "I brought the kids some icecream" and "I brought some icecream to the kids," where "the kids" functions as the indirect object in both sentences, but as the obj. of prep. in only the last sentence. English grammars disagree about the relationship between the I/O and obj. of prep., so don't be too concerned about it.

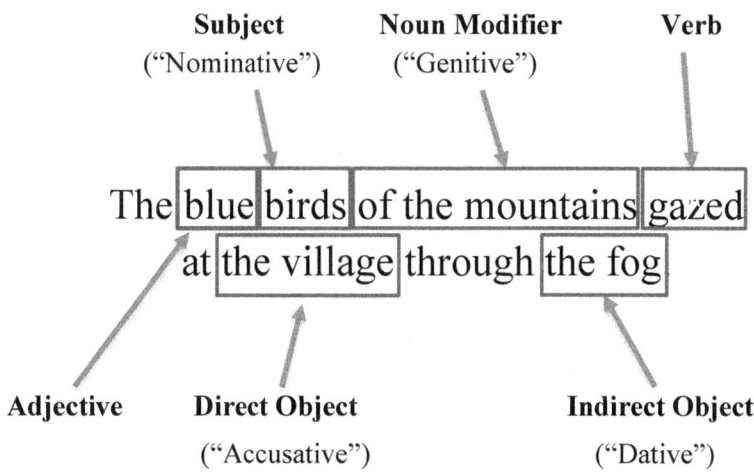

2.2.8   If this sentence were in Greek, "the birds" would have a nominative plural case ending, since the birds are performing the verb of the sentence. "Of the mountains" would have a genitive plural case ending, since they (plural) modify another noun, showing a particular relationship between the two. An alternate translation would be, "The mountains' birds," which would demonstrate a stronger relationship of possession. "The village" would be in the accusative (sg) since it directly receives the action of the verb "gazed." Finally, "the fog" would be in the dative case, since it indirectly receives the action of the subject (sg).

2.3 Grammatical Gender

2.3.1 In addition to *number* (singular or plural) and *case* (nom, gen, dat, acc), Greek nouns also have *gender*. Many languages like Spanish, German, Russian, etc. have grammatical genders for their nouns, such as masculine, feminine, neuter, inanimate, animate, etc. However, English does not have a system of gendered nouns, so this part of learning Greek can be challenging.

2.3.2 Grammatical gender simply classifies nouns into groups (genders), which look and behave differently depending on how the noun is used.[7] Greek has three genders: masculine, feminine, and neuter. This means that every Greek noun is either masculine, feminine, or neuter. (Verbs do not have gender)[8]

2.3.3 Additionally, the gender of a noun never changes. A feminine word is always a feminine word, just as a masculine word is always masculine, and a neuter word always neuter.

2.3.4 How do you tell what the gender of a Greek word is? By the article of the word. If you turn to the end of this chapter you will see a list of words to memorize. But you will also notice one of three articles after the noun in its nominative singular case:

2.3.4.1 *Masculine*: ὁ

2.3.4.2 *Feminine*: ἡ

2.3.4.3 *Neuter*: τό

2.3.5 So, for example, αγαπή has an ἡ after it. So you know that this word is feminine. Here are some more examples:

---

[7] When certain nouns (like personal pronouns, "he," "she") have biological gender ("sex"), grammatical gender usually corresponds to physical gender. But this is not always the case. A prime example is ἀδελφός, which is a masculine word meaning "brother." But most of the time in the NT, it refers to both men and women, so translations often say "brothers and sisters." For various reasons, some American evangelicals became concerned about this topic in the 1990s and early 2000s. For more on this, see D. A. Carson, *The Inclusive Language Debate* (Grand Rapids: Baker, 1998).
[8] Participles, as you will learn, are an exception.

Chapter Two: First and Second Declension Nouns

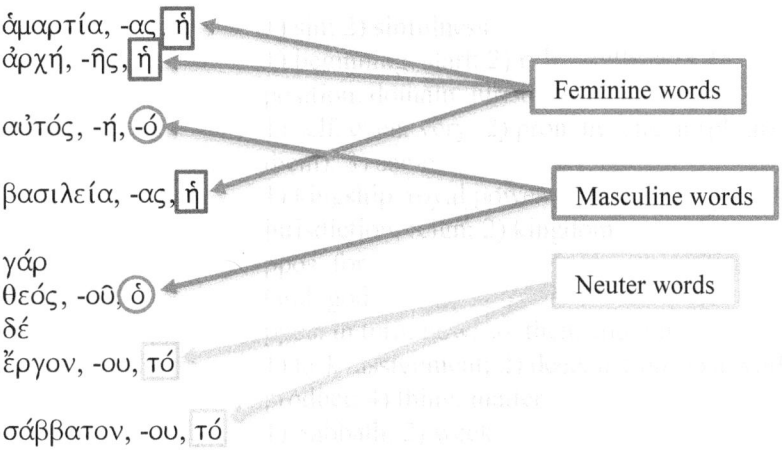

ἁμαρτία, -ας, ἡ
ἀρχή, -ῆς, ἡ
αὐτός, -ή, -ό
βασιλεία, -ας, ἡ
γάρ
θεός, -οῦ, ὁ
δέ
ἔργον, -ου, τό
σάββατον, -ου, τό

2.4 Declension

2.4.1 As noted above, the inflection of a noun is called "declension." The Greek noun system groups the various grammatical categories—case, number, and gender—into three declensions, each with their own rules. Here are the **Three Rules of Declensions**:

2.4.1.1 Nouns that have a stem ending in an α or η are in the *1st declension*. They are called *a*-class nouns and are normally feminine. Example: ἡ ὥρα[9] and ἡ ἀγάπη[10]

2.4.1.2 Nouns that have a stem ending in an o are in the *2nd declension*. They are called *o*-class nouns and are normally masculine and neuter. Example: ὁ καιρός[11] and τό ἔργον.[12]

2.4.1.3 Nouns that have a stem ending in a consonant are in the *3rd declension*. Example: τό ὕδωρ.[13]

2.4.2 All of these grammatical rules and the actual case endings are contained within a single *Table of Case Endings*. The first and

---

[9] Hour, occasion, moment.
[10] Love.
[11] Appointed time, season.
[12] Work, deed, action.
[13] Water.

second declension endings are the focus of this chapter,[14] and like the whole table, they need to be memorized perfectly. You'll find several patterns in this table that will help your memory, like (for example) that neuter words are the same in the nominative and accusative case. You might also see that the datives are the same across the board: singular datives always end in an iota, and plural genitives always end in ων.

	2nd	1st	2nd	3rd	
	Masc	Fem	Neut	M/F	Neut
Sg Nom	ς	–	ν	ς/-	
Sg Gen	υ	ς	υ	ος	ος
Sg Dat	ι	ι	ι	ι	ι
Sg Acc	ν	ν	ν	α/ν	
Pl Nom	ι	ι	α	ες	α
Pl Gen	ων	ων	ων	ων	ων
Pl Dat	ις	ις	ις	σι(ν)	σι(ν)
Pl Acc	υς	ς	α	ας	α

2.4.3 Important Notes About the *Table of Case Endings*

2.4.3.1 The omegas and alphas underlined in the table (ων and α) indicate that these letters absorb the vowel at the end of a noun stem (there is a "contraction").

2.4.3.2 The dash (-) in the singular nominative and singular accusative rows indicates that there is no ending.

2.4.3.3 The singular dative subscripts when possible.[15] This is how the pl. nom. can be distinguished from the dat. sg.

Example: ὥρα + ι = ὥρᾳ

---

[14] This is why the third declension portion is gray.
[15] Recall from chapter 1 that iotas only subscript under vowels, not consonants.

Chapter Two: First and Second Declension Nouns

2.4.4 **Examples of Case Endings in Action**

2.4.4.1 Below are some examples of these case endings at work in simple phrases and sentences. Keep in mind that *case endings determine the function of words more than order.*

The love of God.

ἡ αγαπή θεου.

The son is in the heavens.

ὁ υἱος ἐστιν ἐν τους οὐρανούς.

For the ruler was the Lord of the kingdoms.

ἡ ἀρχή γαρ ἦν ὁ κύριον τῶν βασιλειῶν.

Therefore, on the hour, we went to Galilee.

ὥστε, ἐν ἡ ὥρᾳ, ἐξήλθομεν πρός Γαλιλαίαν.

To him be the glory and now and to the eternal day. Amen.

αὐτῷ ἡ δόξα καὶ νῦν καὶ εἰς ἡμέραν αἰῶνος. *ἀμήν.*[16]

---

[16] 2 Pt 3:18. Italicized or bracketed words in the Greek New Testament indicate a *textual variant,* a difference between manuscripts.

2.5 The Four Rules of First and Second Declension Nouns

2.5.1 1st declension nouns that end in an η in the singular shift to α in the plural. Example: γραφή in the singular nominative changes to γραφαί in the plural nominative.

2.5.2 If a 1st declension word has a stem ending in α where the letter before it is ε, ι or ρ, it will form the genitive and dative with α. In all other cases it will change to η.

Example: ὥρα (nom) changes to ὥρᾳ (dat)

Example: δόξα (nom) changes to δόξῃ (dat)

2.5.3 All neuter words have the same form in the nominative and accusative case.[17]

2.5.4 Greek usually uses a singular verb when the subject is neuter plural. This indicates that the writer is viewing the plural object as one group. (Consider the English phrase, "the Alps is a large mountain range" or "Augustine's *Confessions* is an important book in Western history.") To maintain proper English in our translations, however, the verb will end up being rendered to match the noun. Example:

δοκιμάζετε τὰ πνεύματα [plural] εἰ ἐκ τοῦ θεοῦ ἐστιν [singular verb].
but test the spirits to see whether they are [instead of "it is"] from God.[18]

2.6 The Nominative Case in Detail

2.6.1 As you learned above, the nominative case usually functions as the *subject* of the sentence (performs the action). As such, it is properly called the case of *naming* and *designation*. This is one of three major functions of the nominative:

2.6.1.1 The **Subject** nominative functions as the subject of a finite verb, whether stated or implied.[19] This is the most common use

---

[17] Cf. 2.4.2.
[18] 1 Jn 4:1.

of the nominative. Example: ἠγάπησεν ὁ θεὸς τὸν κόσμον ("<u>God</u> so loved the world," Jn 3:16).

2.6.1.2 The **Predicate** nominative generally functions as the subject of a finite verb, but is joined to it by an equative verb, whether stated or implied. In other words, two nominative nouns are placed next to each other and are equated by the word "is," "become," or "am." Example: καὶ <u>ὁ πατήρ</u> μου ὁ γεωργός ἐστιν ("my <u>Father</u> is the vinegrower," Jn 15:1).[20] You may be wondering: with two nominatives sitting beside each other ("the father" and "the vinegrower"), how do you know which one is the subject and which one is the predicate nominative? One or more of three things will be true about the subject. It will be (1) a pronoun, (2) articular (have an article before it[21]), or (3) be a proper name.

2.6.1.3 **Appositional** nominatives are nominatives beside (in a different position from) other nominatives that function the same way. They are essentially the same as the Predicate nominative but with no verb in mind. One nominative "piggy-backs" on the first nominative's use. In "Paul is an apostle," *apostle* is a PN, but in "Paul the apostle," *apostle* is an apposition to *Paul*. Example: παραγίνεται Ἰωάννης <u>ὁ βαπτιστὴς</u> κηρύσσων ("John <u>the Baptist</u> appeared…proclaiming," Mt 3:1).

---

[19] The verb, as the second half of this grammar teaches, has a voice (active, passive, middle) and type (transitive, intransitive, or equative) that may affect the meaning of the phrase.
[20] It is important to note that the equation between the two nominative nouns does not require complete correspondence (thus, A may = B, but B may not = A in the same sense). See Wallace, *GGBB*, 42.
[21] See the next chapter for more on articles.

2.7 The Genitive Case in Detail

2.7.1 As you learned above, the genitive modifies another noun in a variety of ways. There are ten major ways this occurs:[22]

2.7.1.1 **Descriptive** genitives describe the head noun. In translation, "of" can be replaced with "described by" or "characterized by." Example: μὴ ποιεῖτε τὸν οἶκον τοῦ πατρός μου οἶκον ἐμπορίου. ("Don't make my Father's house a place of business," Jn 2:16, CEB).

2.7.1.2 **Possessive** genitives are possessed (owned) by the head noun. In translation, "of" can be replaced with "belonging to" or "possessed by." The head noun is usually a pronoun (his, her, my, your, their, etc.). Example: αὐτοῦ τὸ ὠτίον ("his ear," Mt 26:51)

2.7.1.3 **Relational** genitives show a family relationship. In translation, "of" can be replaced with "who comes from." Example: Μαρία ἡ Ἰακώβου ("Mary the mother of James," or "James who comes from Mary," Lk 24:10)

2.7.1.4 **Partitive** genitives are the whole of a part.[23] In translation, "of" can be replaced with "which is a part of." Example: τὰ ἡμίσιά μου τῶν ὑπαρχόντων ("half of my possessions," Lk 19:8).

2.7.1.5 **Definitional (Appositional)** genitives[24] are the part (or all) of a whole. In translation, "of" can usually be replaced with "which is" or "who is." Example: ἔλεγεν περὶ τοῦ ναοῦ τοῦ σώματος αὐτοῦ. ("he was speaking of the temple of his body," Jn 2:21)

2.7.1.6 **Attributive** genitives specify an attribute *of* the head noun, and are often used for emphasis. Example: τὸ σῶμα τῆς ἁμαρτίας ("body of sin" or "sinful body," Rom 6:6).

2.7.1.7 **Attributed** genitives are given an attribute *by* the head noun. You can usually know them by omitting "of" from the genitive, forming an adjective that makes sense (the "difficulty of

---

[22] See Wallace, *GGBB*, 72-136, from which most of these examples come.
[23] Also called "Wholative" genitives.
[24] Also called "Genitive of Apposition" and "Epexegetical Genitive."

college" = "difficult college"). Example: τοῦτό μοι καρπὸς ἔργου ("this [will mean the] fruit of labor to me," or "fruitful labor to me," Phil 1:22).

2.7.1.8 **Comparative** genitives specify an attribute of the head noun. In translation, the word "than" or "to" needs to be supplied before the genitive. Example: κρείττων γενόμενος τῶν ἀγγέλων ("[the Son] having become as much superior to the angels," Heb 1:4).

2.7.1.9 **Subjective** genitives function as the subject of the verbal idea implicit in the head noun. The head noun *must* have a possible verbal idea (e.g., the noun "king" could mean the verb "to king," but "blue" could never be "to blue"). Example: οὐδὲ οὕτως ἴση ἦν ἡ μαρτυρία αὐτῶν ("But even on this point their testimony did not agree," or "nor did they testify the same thing," Mk 14:59).[25]

2.7.1.10 **Objective** genitives functions as the direct object implicit in the head noun. In translation, "of" can be replaced with "for," "concerning," "about," "toward," or "against." Example: ἡ δὲ τοῦ πνεύματος βλασφημία οὐκ ἀφεθήσεται. ("but blasphemy of the Spirit will not be forgiven," or "blasphemy against the Spirit," or "blaspheming the spirit," Mt 12:31).

---

[25] One of the most disputed examples involves the genitive "of Christ" and "faith," such as in Rm 3:22 (should it be "faith in Christ" or "the faith/faithfulness of Christ"?). See Wallace, *GGBB*, 114-16.

2.8 The Dative Case in Detail

2.8.1 As you learned above, the dative case primarily functions as the indirect object. This is one of ten major uses[26]:

2.8.1.1 **Indirect Object** datives receive the action of a transitive verb. In translation (and often in the Greek), the words "to" or "for" sometimes precede the dative. Example: καὶ ἔδωκεν ἄν σοι ὕδωρ ζῶν. ("and he would have given [to] you living water," Jn 4:10).

2.8.1.2 **Interest** datives indicate the person interested in the verbal action, usually stressing advantage or disadvantage. In translation (and sometimes in the Greek), the words "to," "for" or "against" precede the dative. Example: τὰ βρώματα τῇ κοιλίᾳ. ("Food is meant for the stomach," 1 Cor 6:13).

2.8.1.3 **Reference** datives qualify a statement that would otherwise not typically be true. In translation (and often in the Greek), the words "with reference to," "about," or "concerning about" precede the dative. Example: πάντα τὰ γεγραμμένα διὰ τῶν προφητῶν τῷ υἱῷ τοῦ ἀνθρώπου. ("everything that is written about the Son of Man by the prophets will be accomplished," Lk 18:31).

2.8.1.4 **Appositional** datives are beside another dative. They "piggy-back" on the first dative's use. Example: ἐν Χριστῷ Ἰησοῦ τῷ κυρίῳ ἡμῶν. ("in Jesus Christ our Lord," Rom 6:23).

2.8.1.5 **Spherical** datives indicate the sphere or location in which something occurs. In translation, the words "in the sphere of" or "in the realm of" precede the dative. Example: Χριστὸς ἅπαξ περὶ ἁμαρτιῶν ἔπαθεν, δίκαιος ὑπὲρ ἀδίκων, ἵνα ὑμᾶς προσαγάγῃ τῷ θεῷ, θανατωθεὶς μὲν σαρκί. ("For Christ also suffered once for sins once for all, the righteous for the unrighteous, in order to bring you to God. He was put put to death in the flesh," 1 Pt 3:18).

---

[26] See Wallace, *GGBB*, 137-175, from which most of these examples come.

2.8.1.6 **Temporal** datives indicate when something occurs. Example: προσεύχεσθε δὲ ἵνα μὴ γένηται ἡ φυγὴ ὑμῶν χειμῶνος μηδὲ σαββάτῳ ("Pray that your flight may not be in winter or on a sabbath," Mt 24:20).

2.8.1.7 **Associative** datives indicate an association. In translation, the words "in association with" precede the dative. Example: οἱ δὲ ἄνδρες οἱ συνοδεύοντες αὐτῷ ("the men who were traveling with him," Acts 9:7).

2.8.1.8 **Adverbial (Manner)** datives indicate how something occurs. In translation, the words "with" or "in" often precede the dative. Example: παρρησίᾳ λαλεῖ ("he speaks with boldness," or "speaking openly" Jn 7:26).

2.8.1.9 **Instrumental** datives indicate the means or instrument used. In translation, the words "by means of" or "by" precede the dative. Example: δεδάμασται τῇ φύσει τῇ ἀνθρωπίνῃ ("has been tamed by the human species," Js 3:7).

2.8.1.10 **Causal** datives indicate the cause or basis of the verb's action. In translation, the words "because of" or "on the basis of" often precede the dative. Example: ἐγὼ δὲ λιμῷ ὧδε ἀπόλλυμαι. ("but I perish here because of hunger," or "but here I am dying of hunger," Lk 15:17).

2.9 The Accusative Case in Detail

2.9.1 As you learned above, the accusative case usually functions as the direction object. This is one of five functions of the accusative[27]:

2.9.1.1 **Direct Object** accusatives receive the action of a transitive verb.[28] Example: οὐκ ἦλθον καλέσαι <u>δικαίους</u> ἀλλὰ <u>ἁμαρτωλούς</u> ("I have not come to call the <u>righteous</u> but <u>sinners</u>," Mk 2:17).

2.9.1.2 **Person-Thing** accusatives are two direct objects, one a person and the other a thing. Example: ἐκεῖνος <u>ὑμᾶς</u> διδάξει <u>πάντα</u> ("[he] will teach <u>you</u> <u>everything</u>," Jn 14:26).

2.9.1.3 **Object-Complement** accusatives are two accusatives, a direct object and another accusative that complements it. Example: λογίζεσθε <u>ἑαυτοὺς</u> εἶναι <u>νεκροὺς</u> μὲν τῇ ἁμαρτίᾳ ("consider <u>yourselves</u>[obj] <u>dead</u>[comp] to sin," Rom 6:11).[29]

2.9.1.4 **Infinitive Subject** accusatives function as the subject of the infinitive.[30] Sometimes this can involve one accusative, and sometimes two. In the sentence, "Dad wanted me to get some food," "me" is both the direct object of "wanted" and the subject of the infinitive "to get." Example: ινώσκειν καὶ ἀπέστειλεν τοὺς <u>δούλους</u> αὐτοῦ καλέσαι ("He sent his <u>slaves</u> to call," Mt 22:3).

2.9.1.5 **Appositional** accusatives are beside another accusative. They "piggy-back" on the first accusative's use. Example: Πίστευσον ἐπὶ τὸν κύριον <u>Ἰησοῦν</u> ("believe on the Lord <u>Jesus</u>," Acts 16:31).

---

[27] See Wallace, *GGBB,* 176-205, from which most of these examples come.
[28] A transitive verb has an object (e.g., "she drove the car"), as opposed to an intransitive verb which doesn't (e.g., "she drove").
[29] Like the Predicate Nominative (see above), you can tell which accusative is the object if it is (1) a pronoun, (2) articular, or (3) a proper name.
[30] The infinitive form of a verb is "to learn," "to talk," "to" etc., instead of "learned" or "learning," etc. An example of this kind of accusative in English would be "he challenged me <u>to climb</u> the route," where "me" is the direct object of both "challenged" and "to debate" (the infinitive).

Chapter Two: First and Second Declension Nouns

Vocabulary

ἀγάπη, -ης, ἡ	1) affection, esteem, love; 2) love feast
ἄλλος, -η, -ο	other
ἁμαρτία, -ας, ἡ	1) sin; 2) sinfulness
ἀρχή, -ῆς, ἡ	1) beginning, start; 2) ruler, authority; 3) position, domain, jurisdiction
αὐτός, -ή, -ό	1) self, even, very; 2) pron. he, she, it (pl. they, them); 3) same
βασιλεία, -ας, ἡ	1) kingship, royal power/rule/reign, royal jurisdiction, reign; 2) kingdom
γάρ	ppos.[31] for
δέ	ppos. in turn, now, so, then, and, but
ἔργον, -ου, τό	1) task, assignment; 2) deed, action; 3) a work, product; 4) thing, matter
εἶ	you are (2nd pers. sg. εἰμι)
εἶπεν	he/she/it said (3rd pers. sg. aor. λέγω)
εἰμί	am; are, is, was, were, will be
εἰς	prep. w. acc. 1) into, to, toward, for, with a view to, against, about, in reference to, at, in, via, by, up to, on; 2) to, until
εἰσίν	they are (pl. εἰμι)
ἐν	prep. w. dat. 1) in, on, at, among, by; 2) in; 3) with, along with, with the help of, through; 5) because of, on account of; 6) in, while, when
ἐστίν	he/she/it is (3rd pers. sg. εἰμι)
ἐξουσία, -ας, ἡ	1) authority, right, jurisdiction, privilege; 2) authority
εὐαγγέλιον, -ου, τό	good news
ἦν	he/she/it was (3rd pers. sg. impf. εἰμι)
Ἰησοῦς, -οῦ, ὁ	Jesus, Joshua
καιρός, -οῦ, ὁ	1) time; 2) time, period
κύριος, -ου, ὁ	1) owner, lord, master; 2) lord, master, sir
μή	not; a) not, that…not, lest, so that…not; b) not…not x; c) not, not ever

---

[31] A *postpositive* is a word that comes first in English, but comes *after* another word in Greek. For example, εἰμι γάρ τόν κύριον would be translated "<u>For</u> I am the Lord" instead of "I am for the Lord." The two most common postpostives are γάρ and δέ.

νῦν	1) now, just now; 2) as the matter now stands, now, but now, but as it is, as a matter of fact
ὁ, ἡ, τό	1) dem. pron. this one, that one; 2) art. the
ὅτι	1) dem. pron. (namely) that; 3) ""; 4) because, for, that, inasmuch, why?
οὐ, οὐκ, οὐχ	a) no; b-c) not
οὐρανός, -ου, ὁ	1) heaven, sky; 2) heaven; 3) God
οὗτος	1) dem. pron. sg. this, he/she/it/they, pl. these, sg. this fellow; 2) adj. this
σύ	2nd pers. pron. you., you (persons), your
υἱός, -οῦ, ὁ	1) son, descendant, offspring, foal; 2) son, person, children, child, people.
ὥστε	1) for this reason, therefore, (and) so; 2) so that, for the purpose of, with a view to, in order that
ὥρα, -ας, ἡ	1) hour, time, (a/the) time; 2) time

Chapter Three: Articles, Prepositions and Third Declension Nouns

3 Articles, Prepositions, and Third Declension Nouns

3.1 Articles

3.1.1 Like English, Greek has articles.[1] The definite article in English is the word "the," and the indefinite article is "a" or "an." These English articles have no case, number, or gender.

3.1.2 Greek is much different. There is no distinction between definite and indefinite articles. Additionally, Greek articles are *declinable*, meaning that they fall into declensions having case, number and gender. (Note that we have already learned the nominative singular form of the article—masculine ὁ, feminine ἡ, and neuter τό.) This is because the article of any Greek word will match the case, number, and gender of the noun it is modifying.[2]

3.1.3 Examples:

3.1.3.1 ὁ λογός

3.1.3.2 τούς λογούς

3.1.3.3 τού λογού

3.1.3.4 τάς ὥρας

3.1.3.5 ἡ ὥρα

---

[1] Articles should not be confused with *particles*, which are conjunctions, prepositions, and adverbs.
[2] As you will also notice, the article will *sound* the same as the case ending.

3.1.4　*The Table of Articles*

	2nd Masc	1st Fem	2nd Neut
Sg Nom	ὁ	ἡ	τό
Sg Gen	τοῦ	τῆς	τοῦ
Sg Dat	τῷ	τῇ	τῷ
Sg Acc	τόν	τήν	τό
Pl Nom	οἱ	αἱ	τά
Pl Gen	τῶν	τῶν	τῶν
Pl Dat	τοῖς	ταῖς	τοῖς
Pl Acc	τούς	τάς	τά

3.1.5　Articles are crucial to remember when reviewing vocabulary words because they immediately tell you the word's gender. Recall the following examples (mostly) from the last chapter (2.3.5):

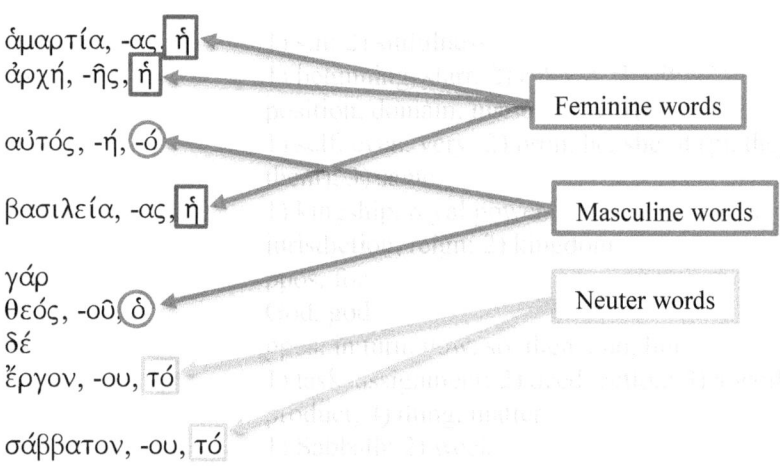

Chapter Three: Articles, Prepositions and Third Declension Nouns

3.1.6 Words that have the article are *articular*, and words without the article are *anarthrous*.

3.1.7 The *Table of Articles* and the first and second declension sections of the *Table of Case Endings* are very similar. Observing these similarities may aid your memorization:

Case Endings			Articles		
Masc	Fem	Neut	Masc	Fem	Neut
ς	–	ν	ὁ	ἡ	τό
υ	ς	υ	τοῦ	τῆς	τοῦ
ι	ι	ι	τῷ	τῇ	τῷ
ν	ν	ν	τόν	τήν	τό
ι	ι	α	οἱ	αἱ	τά
ων	ων	ων	τῶν	τῶν	τῶν
ις	ις	ις	τοῖς	ταῖς	τοῖς
υς	ς	α	τούς	τάς	τά

3.1.8 Greek articles are not always translated as "the." Instead, articles can be used for *emphasis*. Example: in John 1, καὶ ὁ λόγος ἦν πρός τόν θεόν is not translated "and the Word was with *the* God," even though the article (τόν) is before the word God. It is used to emphasize something; "and the Word was with *GOD*."

3.1.9 Likewise, the Greek article can sometimes be included in a translation when it is absent. Example: καὶ πῦρ ἐξῆλθεν παρὰ κυρίου is translated "and fire came from the Lord," and not "and fire came from Lord."[3]

3.1.10 Since the Greek article functions differently than the English article, it is necessary to review the three uses of the article.

---

[3] Num 16:35 (LXX).

3.1.11 The Three Common Uses of the Article

3.1.11.1 As a Pronoun

3.1.11.1.1 *Personal pronoun* (he, she, it). Example: Οἱ δὲ εἶπαν πρὸς αὐτόν ("Then they said to him," Lk 5:33).

3.1.11.1.2 *Relative pronoun* (who, which). Example: Πάτερ ἡμῶν ὁ ἐν τοῖς οὐρανοῖς ("Our Father who is in heaven," Mt 6:9, NASB).

3.1.11.1.3 *Possessive pronoun* (her, his). Example: Οἱ ἄνδρες, ἀγαπᾶτε τὰς γυναῖκας ("Husbands, love your wives," Eph 5:23).

3.1.11.2 To Distinguish (dependent/modifying use).[4]

3.1.11.2.1 *Individualizing articles* distinguish one individual from another either through (1) identification (Lk 4:20, Acts 10:9), (2) anaphora[5] (Jn 4:40; 4:50; Js 2:14), (3) deixis[6] (Mt 14:15; John 19:5), (4) *par excellence*[7] (Jn 1:21; 1 Cor 3:13; Lk 18:13), (5) uniqueness (Mk 13:24; Jn 1:29), (6) popularity (Gal 4:22; Js 1:1), or (7) abstraction (Rom 12:9)

3.1.11.2.2 *Categorical articles* are generic articles that distinguish one class from another (instead of distinguishing a particular object from a larger class). Example: ἔστω σοι ὥσπερ ὁ ἐθνικὸς καὶ ὁ τελώνης. ("let such a one be to you as a Gentile and a tax-collector," Mt 18:17).

---

[4] The images below comes from *GGBB,* 227 (Chart 18) and 230 (Chart 19).

[5] An *anaphora* is a type of expression whose reference depends on another referential element. For example, "Are you the guy who wrecked his car"? The "guy" refers back to something that had been earlier introduced.

[6] *Deixis* refers to when understanding the meaning of words in an utterance requires contextual information. A *deictic* article points out an object who is *present* at the moment of speaking.

[7] *Par excellence* (French, "by excellence") indicates the extreme in a class.

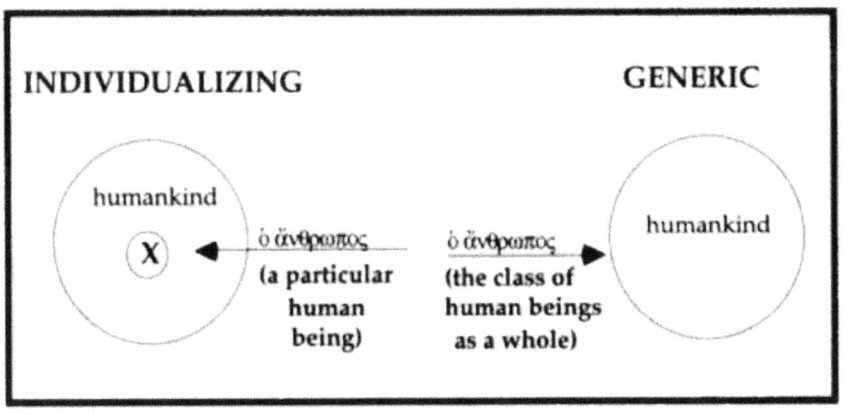

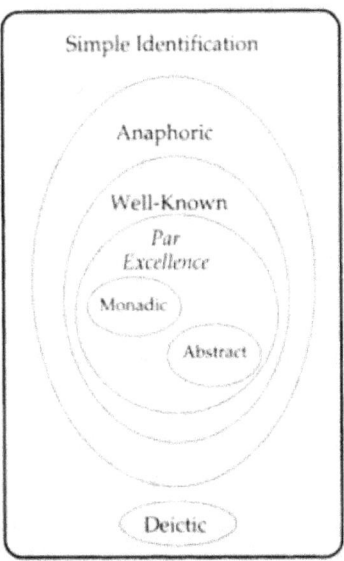

3.1.11.1 **To Substitute** (independent use)

3.1.11.1.1 Articles can substitute for adverbs, adjectives, participles, infinitives, genitive word or phrase, prepositional phrase, or clause/quotation). Example (substituting for a prepositional phrase): οἱ ἐκ περιτομῆς ("those who were circumcised," Acts 11:2, NASB).

3.1.11.1.2 The big indicator of whether or not an article is functioning independently is if it is not immediately standing beside another noun. (See example above.)

3.2 Prepositions

3.2.1 Prepositions are words that indicate the relationship between two different nouns. The relationship is usually spatial (answering "where?") or temporal (answering "when?"). Example: in the English sentence, "the student is under the table," the word "under" is the preposition, demonstrating a relationship between "student" and "table." In the Greek sentence, καὶ ὁ θεὸς ἐν αὐτῷ μένει (and God remains in him) ἐν is the preposition.

3.2.2 The word following a preposition—the *object of the preposition*—is usually in the dative or genitive case. Example: καὶ ὁ θεὸς ἐν αὐτῷ μένει.

3.2.3 The preposition and object of preposition together form a *prepositional phrase*. Using the same example from above, this would be ἐν αὐτῷ ("in him").

3.2.4 Since prepositions essentially function the same as key words for the dative case (to, in, with) and the genitive case (of, from, by), prepositions replace those key words. Example: καὶ ὁ θεὸς ἐν αὐτῷ μένει should be translated "and God remains in him," and not "and God remains to in him." Likewise, παρὰ κυρίου means "from the Lord," not "from of the Lord."

3.2.5 Prepositions are not inflected. They are not affected by case endings, gender, or number. παρὰ always stays παρὰ and ἐν always stays ἐν, no matter what.

3.2.6 However, while prepositions do not inflect or conjugate, they do undergo *elision*. When a preposition *ends* with a vowel and the following word *begins* with a vowel, the vowel on the end of the preposition may fall out and be replaced by an apostrophe. Example: μετὰ αὐτοῦ becomes μετ' αὐτοῦ. Elision obviously makes speaking and reading much smoother, because instead of pronouncing both vowels, only one has to be pronounced.

3.2.7 Like some nouns, prepositions can also have multiple meanings. Example: διὰ means "through" when the object of the preposition is in the genitive case, but it can mean "because of" when the object of the preposition is in the accusative case.

These differences must be memorized as part of vocabulary entries.[8]

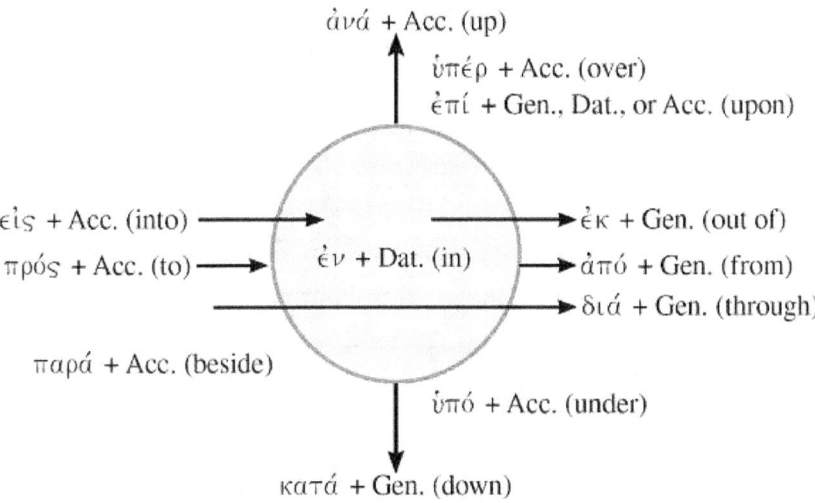

---

[8] The image below comes from Black, *Learn to Read New Testament Greek*, 60.

3.3 Third Declension Nouns

3.3.1 Third declension nouns have stems that end in a consonant.

Example: καρπὸν χειλέων ὁμολογούντων τῷ <u>ὀνόματι</u> αὐτοῦ[9]
("…the fruit of lips that confess his name")
Example: ἀλλὰ δοκιμάζετε τὰ <u>πνεύματα</u> εἰ ἐκ τοῦ θεοῦ ἐστιν[10]
("but test the spirits to see whether they are from God")

3.3.2 *Table of Case Endings*

| | 2nd | 1st | 2nd | 3rd | |
	Masc	Fem	Neut	M/F	Neut
Sg Nom	ς		ν	ς / –	–
Sg Gen	υ	ς	υ	ος	ος
Sg Dat	ι	ι	ι	ι	ι
Sg Acc	ν	ν	ν	α / ν	–
Pl Nom	ι	ι	α	ες	α
Pl Gen	ων	ων	ων	ων	ων
Pl Dat	ις	ις	ις	σι(ν)	σι(ν)
Pl Acc	υς	ς	α	ας	α

3.3.3 Notice that the singular nominative and singular accusative can have one of two different endings in the M/F column. Either gender can have either ending.

---

[9] Heb 13:5b.
[10] 1 Jn 4:1.

Chapter Three: Articles, Prepositions and Third Declension Nouns

3.3.4 Unlike most first and second declension nouns, third declension nouns often contract with case endings because they end in a consonant. Recall the *Table of Stops and Fricatives*:

	Stops	Fricatives		
		Hard	Soft	
Labial	π	φ	β	ψ
Velar	κ	χ	γ	ξ
Dental	τ	θ	δ	σ

When a σ is added to a Labial letter, the two form a ψ.
When a σ is added to a Velar letter, the two form a ξ.
When a σ is added to a Dental letter, the two condense into a σ.
Therefore, σαρκ + σι = σαρξι.

3.3.5 *This is why the genitive case ending (with stem vowel) is included in a vocabulary entry,* and why it is so important to remember. The vocabulary entry σάρξ, σαρκός, ἡ has the three basic elements: nominative singular word, genitive singular ending (w/stem vowel), and the article. Since the third declension stem (σαρκ) reacts with third declension nominative singular case ending (ς) to form ξ, the only possible way to identify the actual stem of the word is to drop off the genitive case ending. Hence, σαρκός - ός = σαρκ (stem). So, without knowing the genitive case ending, it would be virtually impossible to find out the stem of a third declension word.

3.3.6 Test yourself using the vocabulary list at the end of this chapter:

What is the stem of ὀνόμα? = ὀνόματ

What is the stem of σὰρξ? = σὰρκ

What is the stem of σῶμά? = σῶμάτ

3.3.7 **The Five Rules of the Third Declension**

3.3.7.1 The iota does not subscript in the third declension since iotas can only subscript under a vowel.

3.3.7.2 *A constantal iota stem* is a feminine word that ends in an ι where the ι often changes to an ε. Example: the genitive of πίστις is πίστεως.

3.3.7.3 A movable nu (ν) is an optional ν for when the next word begins with a vowel. Example: in English we say "a<u>n</u> apple," not "a apple." The same goes for Greek. ἐστί(ν) has a movable ν that is present when the first letter of the next word is a vowel. The movable ν is standard for the 3rd declension dative plural (see the table above).

3.3.7.4 A ν always drops out when followed by a σ. Example: τιν + σ = τίς.

3.3.7.5 A τ always drops out when followed by a σ or if it stands alone at the end of a word. Example: ὀνοματ + σι = ὀνομασι, and ὀνοματ = ὀνομα.

3.3.8 Having learned these five rules of third declension, you now know *The Twelve Grammatical Rules of Greek Nouns*!

Chapter Three: Articles, Prepositions and Third Declension Nouns

The Twelve Grammatical Rules of Greek Nouns

1. Nouns that have a stem ending in an α or η are in the 1st declension.
2. Nouns that have a stem ending in an o are in the 2nd declension.
3. Nouns that have a stem ending in a consonant are in the 3rd declension.
4. 1st declension nouns that end in an η in the singular shift to α in the plural.
5. If a 1st declension word has a stem ending in α where the letter before it is ε, ι or ρ, it will form the genitive and dative with α. In all other cases it will change to η.
6. All neuter words have the same form in the nominative and accusative case.
7. Greek usually uses a singular verb when the subject is neuter plural.
8. The iota does not subscript in the third declension since iotas can only subscript under a vowel.
9. *A constantal iota stem* is a feminine word that ends in an ι where the ι often changes to an ε.
10. A movable nu (ν) is an optional ν for when the next word begins with a vowel.
11. A ν always drops out when followed by a σ.
12. A τ always drops out when followed by a σ or if it stands alone at the end of a word.

Vocabulary

ἅγιος, -ία, -ιον	holy
ἀλλά	but, on the other hand, yet, nevertheless, indeed, certaintly
ἀνήρ, ἀνδρός, ὁ	man
ἀπό [ἀπ', ἀφ']	prep. w. gen. from
διά	prep. through; a) w. gen. through; b) w. acc. through, because of
εἰ	1) if; 2) if, whether
εἷς, μία, ἕν	one; 1) one, one and the same, first; 2) someone
ἐκ, ἐξ	prep. w. gen: a) from, out of; by, from *x* on; b) at; c) for
ἤδη	adv. now, already
ἡμέρα, -ας, ἡ	1) day; 2) day(s); time
θάλασσα, -ης, ἡ	1) sea; 2) lake
θάνατος, -ου, ὁ	death
ἵνα	1) in order that; 2-3) that
Ἰωάννης, -ου, ὁ	John
κατά	prep. w. gen. and w. acc. 1) throughout, down (from/along), along, toward, to, as far as; 2) w. gen. (swear) by; 3) w. gen. against; 4-5) w. acc. in line with, in accordance with, in keeping with; 6) w. acc. for, as a result of; 7) w. acc. according to
λέγω	I a) say; b) refer to, talk (about), mention; c) call, name, a.k.a., mean(s)
μετά [μετ', μεθ']	prep. 1) w. gen. with, amid, among, in the company of, along with; 2) w. acc: after, behind
ὄνομα, -ατος, τό	1) name; 2) person
οἶκος, -ου, ὁ	1) house, home, dwelling; 2) house, household, family
οἰκία, -ας, ἡ	1) house, 2) household, family
ὄχλος, -ου, ὁ	crowd
παρά	prep. 1) w. gen. from (the side of); 2) w. dat. with, in association with, in the presence of, among, beside, next to, near; 3) w. acc. alongside, near, at, by, beside, in contrast to, in preference to, contrary to, beyond
πᾶς, πᾶσα, πᾶν	all, whole, each, every(one/thing/body), every kind/sort (of)

Chapter Three: Articles, Prepositions and Third Declension Nouns

πατήρ, πατρός, ὁ	1) father, parents; 2) ancestor, forebear; 3-5) father
περί	prep. about; a) w. gen. about, concerning, for; b) w. acc. with, in connection with, about, around, near
πίστις, -εως, ἡ	1) faithfulness, fidelity, promise, guarantee, pledge; 2) faith, trust, confidence, conviction
πρός	prep. 1) w. acc. to, toward, for, next to, at, against, with a view to, in view of, with, before, relating to, pertaining to, in reference to, in keeping with, regarding, relative to, compared to, with x in mind, for the benefit of x, against; 2) w. gen. in the interest of; 3) w. dat. at, close by, near
σάρξ, σαρκός, ἡ	1) flesh, human being, person; 2) old self
σύν	prep. w. dat. with, along with, including, as well as, besides/not only all this
σῶμα, -ατος, τό	1) body, corpse; 2) body
τέκνον, -ου, τό	1) child; 2) descendants, posterity, son; 3) child
τις, τι	pron. someone, anyone, one, a certain one, a somebody, certain (ones), some, something, anything, any, a certain
τίς, τί	1) who?, what?, why?, what, which; 2) why?, how!
ὕδωρ, ὕδατος, τό	water
ὑπέρ	prep. 1) w. gen. for, in behalf of, in the interest of, in place of, instead of, in the name of, because of, for the sake, about, concerning, with regard to; 2) w. acc. above, beyond, over, more than, than, even more
ὑπό [ὑπ', ὑφ']	prep. 1) w. gen. by, at the hands of, from; 2) w. acc. below, under, next to, at, about, subject to
φῶς, φωτός, τό	1) light; 2) torch, lamp, fire, sun, heavenly bodies
χάρις, -ιτος, ἡ	1) favor, grace; 2) favor, grace, beneficence, blessing; 3) expression of requital, thanks

4 Adjectives and Adverbs

4.1 Introduction

4.1.1 An *adjective* is a word that modifies a substantive. Adjectives can function as attributes, predicates, and even nouns.

4.1.2 Adjectives are *declinable*. They have case, number, and gendre. Therefore, just like the article of a noun must match the case, number, and gender of the noun, so too the adjective must match the case, number, and gender of the noun it is modifying.

4.1.3 If there is no word to modify, like in the instance of a *substantival* adjective, the case is determined by its function in the sentence while its gender and number are determined by what it stands for.

4.2 Attributive Function

4.2.1 Attributive adjectives function as attributes (modifiers) of nouns. This is the most common use of adjectives. Example:

4.2.1.1 "I love the <u>new</u> Greek textbook."

4.2.1.2 <u>ὁ κακός</u> δοῦλος means "the <u>bad</u> slave."

4.3 Predicate Function

4.3.1 Predicate adjectives say something about the subject. The verb "to be" (εἰμί) is either stated or implied. Example:

4.3.1.1 God <u>is good</u>.

4.3.1.2 ὁ ἀδελφός <u>πιστός</u> = "the brother <u>is faithful</u>."

4.4 Substantival Function

4.4.1 Substantival adjectives function as substantives.[1] Since there is no noun to modify, the case of a substantival adjective is determined by its function in the sentence while its gender and number are contextually determined by what it stands for. Example:

4.4.1.1 "The <u>smart</u> and <u>intelligent</u> study Greek."

4.4.1.2 παντὸς <u>ἀγαθοῦ</u> = of every <u>good thing</u>[2]

4.5 Determining the Function of an Adjective

4.5.1 The key to determining the function of an adjective is by looking at the article.

4.5.1.1 If there is an article *before the adjective*, the adjective functions *attributively*. The word order does not matter. Example: ὁ κακός δοῦλος[3] and ὁ δοῦλος ὁ κακός[4] means "the bad slave."[5]

4.5.1.2 If there is an article *before the noun*, but not before the adjective, the adjective functions *predicately*. Example: πιστός ὁ ἀδελφός[6] and ὁ ἀδελφός πιστός[7] mean "the brother is faithful."

4.5.1.3 If there is no noun for the adjective to modify, then the adjective functions substantivaly. Example: ὁ ἀγαθός means "the good (man/person)."

4.5.1.4 If there is no article at all, context determines the function of the adjective. Example: κακός δοῦλος or δοῦλος κακός can mean either "a bad slave" or "a slave is bad."

---

[1] Recall from chapter 2 that a substantive is "a word or group of words that function as a noun."
[2] Phil 1:6.
[3] This is called the *first attributive position* (article-adjective-noun).
[4] This is called the *second attributive position* (article-noun-article-adjective).
[5] You will generally not see "ὁ κακός ὁ δοῦλος." There is, however, a *third attributive position* (noun-article-adjective), that is rarely used (e.g., Lk 15:22, Jn 1:18).
[6] This is called the *first predicate position* (adjective-article-noun). See Mt 5:9, 1 Jn 3:10.
[7] This is called the *second predicate position* (article-noun-adjective). See Js 2:26; 1 Pt 2:12.

4.6 Patterns of Adjectives

4.6.1 As mentioned above, adjectives are *declinable*, meaning that they correspond to the three declensions of the noun case ending system. This makes them easy to memorize since they share all the endings of nouns. However, since they are not actually nouns themselves, they do have some unique patterns. Below are the four major patterns of adjective endings, divided by declension.

2-1-2 Pattern: ἀγαθός, -ή, -όν — good, useful.

	Masc (2)	Fem (1)	Neut (2)
Singular Nominative	ἀγαθός	ἀγαθή	ἀγαθόν
Singular Genitive	ἀγαθοῦ	ἀγαθῆς	ἀγαθοῦ
Singular Dative	ἀγαθῷ	ἀγαθῇ	ἀγαθῷ
Singular Accusative	ἀγαθόν	ἀγαθήν	ἀγαθόν
Plural Nominative	ἀγαθοί	ἀγαθαί	ἀγαθά
Plural Genitive	ἀγαθῶν	ἀγαθῶν	ἀγαθῶν
Plural Dative	ἀγαθοῖς	ἀγαθαῖς	ἀγαθοῖς
Plural Accusative	ἀγαθούς	ἀγαθάς	ἀγαθά

3-1-3 Pattern: πᾶς, πᾶσα, πᾶν — each, every, all.[8]

	Masc (3)	Fem (1)	Neut (3)
Singular Nominative	πᾶς	πᾶσᾰ	πᾶν
Singular Genitive	παντός	πάσης	παντός
Singular Dative	παντί	πάσῃ	παντί
Singular Accusative	πάντᾰ	πᾶσαν	πᾶν
Plural Nominative	πάντες	πᾶσαι	πάντᾰ
Plural Genitive	πάντων	πασῶν	πάντων
Plural Dative	πᾶσι(ν)	πάσαις	πᾶσι(ν)
Plural Accusative	πάντᾰς	πάσας	πάντᾰ

---

[8] εἷς, μία, ἕν (one) is another common 3-1-3 adjective.

Chapter Four: Adjectives and Adverbs

2-2 Pattern: ἄδικος, -ον, — unjust.[9]

	Masc/Fem (2)	Neut (2)
Singular Nominative	ἄδικος	ἄδικον
Singular Genitive	ἀδίκου	ἀδίκου
Singular Dative	ἀδίκῳ	ἀδίκῳ
Singular Accusative	ἄδικον	ἄδικον
Plural Nominative	ἄδικοι	ἄδικᾰ
Plural Genitive	ἀδίκων	ἀδίκων
Plural Dative	ἀδίκοις	ἀδίκοις
Plural Accusative	ἀδίκους	ἄδικᾰ

3-3 Pattern: ἀληθής, -ές — true, truthful.[10]

	Masc/Fem (3)	Neut (3)
Singular Nominative	ἀληθής	ἀληθές
Singular Genitive	ἀληθοῦς	ἀληθοῦς
Singular Dative	ἀληθεῖ	ἀληθεῖ
Singular Accusative	ἀληθῆ	ἀληθές
Plural Nominative	ἀληθεῖς	ἀληθῆ
Plural Genitive	ἀληθῶν	ἀληθῶν
Plural Dative	ἀληθέσι(ν)	ἀληθέσι(ν)
Plural Accusative	ἀληθεῖς	ἀληθῆ

---

[9] Adjectives in this category use one set of endings when modifying a masculine or a feminine word, and another set of endings when modifying a neuter word. For more on the contractions involved in 3-3 adjectives, see Mounce, *Morphology*, 234ff.

[10] Since this adjective is a 3-3, the adjective has a stem ending in a consonant (in this case, it ends in εσ).

4.6.2   Thus, a 2-1-2 pattern = 2nd decl—1st decl—2nd decl, having masculine endings in the first column, the feminine in the second, and the neuter in the third. A 2-2 pattern has only second declension endings (m/n). The same idea goes for 3-1-3 (m/f-f-m/f) and 3-3 (m/f-neut).

4.6.3   Just like with nouns, adjectives follow the same declension rules: a 1st declension adjective has a stem ending in an α or η; a 2nd declension adjective has a stem ending in an o; a 3rd declension adjective has a stem ending in a consonant.

4.6.4   Adjectives are easy to learn since the vocabulary entries tell you the pattern. If an adjective vocab entry only contains two items, you already know it's either a 2-2 or 3-3 pattern, and if it has three items it's either a 2-1-2 or a 3-1-3. Example: τίς, τί is a 3-3. So, if you know the *Table of Case Endings* and know the lexical form of an adjective, you already know its forms.

4.7   Adjectival Degrees

4.7.1   Adjectives also possess one of three major degrees:

   a. *Positive Degree* — "large" (μέγας)
   b. *Comparative Degree* — "larger" (μεῖζον)
   c. *Superlative Degree* — "largest" (μεῖζον)

4.7.2   As you can see, NT Greek (around the first century) combined the form of the comparative and the superlative so that they both appear to be the same. Translations therefore disagree in places:

ὅταν δὲ αὐξηθῇ μεῖζον τῶν λαχάνων ἐστὶν…
but when it has grown it is the greatest/largest of shrubs (NRSV, NIV, CEB)[11]
but when it is full grown, it is larger than the garden plants (NASB; ESV)

---

[11] Mt 13:32.

But usually they agree, as in the following:

Ζῶν γὰρ ὁ λόγος τοῦ θεοῦ καὶ ἐνεργὴς καὶ <u>τομώτερος</u> ὑπὲρ πᾶσαν μάχαιραν δίστομον.
For the word of God is living, active and <u>sharper</u> than any two-edged sword.[12]

4.7.3   The positive degree is a focus on *kind*. The "nice man" is what *kind* of man? A *nice* man.

4.7.4   The difference between the comparative and the superlative is not of kind or degree, but of number. Comparatives compare *two* things ("The pen is mightier than the sword"), while superlative adjectives (usually) compare *three* or more ("The pen is the mightiest of all weapons").

4.7.5   Comparative and superlative adjectives may sometimes be *elative*, which (like positive adjectives) focuses on kind rather than degree. Elatives describe an *intensification* of the positive notion (usually translating with the word "very"). So, for example, instead of saying "smaller" or "smallest," the elative would be rendered "very small."

4.7.5.1   A potential example[13] using the comparative: ὃς ὤφθη ἐπὶ ἡμέρας <u>πλείους</u> = "who appeared for <u>very many</u> days" (instead of just "many days").

4.7.5.2   An example using the superlative: καὶ συνάγεται πρὸς αὐτὸν ὄχλος <u>πλεῖστος</u> = "Such a <u>very large</u> crowd gathered around him" (instead of "greater crowd" or "greatest crowd").

---

[12] Heb 4:12.
[13] I use "potential" example because no known translation agrees with Wallace's rendering here (including the NET, where Wallace is the New Testament senior editor!).

4.8 Adverbs

4.8.1 *Adverbs* are words that modify or describe verbs. They are usually indeclinable. In English, it is typical to add "ly" to a verb or adjective to create an adverb. Example: "She slowly drove home." "Slowly" is describing how she "drove" home.

4.8.2 Greek works the same, typically ending with –ως. Example: Καλῶς ἐπροφήτευσεν Ἡσαΐας περὶ ὑμῶν τῶν ὑποκριτῶν[14] ("Isaiah prophesied rightly about you hypocrites.")

Noun (Nominal Cognate)	Verb (Verbal Cognate)	Adjective	Adverb
δικαιοσύνη, ης ("righteousness")	δικαιόω ("make right")	δίκαιος, -α, -ον ("righteous")	δικαίως ("righteously")
κακοποιός, οῦ ("evil doer") κακία, ας ("badness")	κακοποιέω ("do bad")	κακός, -ή, -όν ("bad")	κακῶς ("badly")
καλοδιδάσκαλος, ου ("good teacher")	καλοποιέω ("do good")	καλός, -ή, -όν ("good")	Καλῶς ("rightly")

4.8.3 According to Decker, καὶ is used as an adverb ("even," "also," "namely") when not joining two grammatically equal items.[15] Most lexicographers, however, do not typically refer to this second semantic use ("adjunctive"[16]) as adverbial, but simply as "emphatic"[17] or "intensive,"[18] often modifying other words besides verbs.

---

[14] Mk 7:6.
[15] Decker, *Reading*, 106.
[16] *CL*, 183.
[17] Liddell, *IGEL*.
[18] *CL*, 183.

Chapter Four: Adjectives and Adverbs

Vocabulary

ἀγαθός, -ή, -όν	beneficial, useful, helpful, good
ἀγαπητός, -ή, -όν	esteemed, dear, beloved
ἀδελφός, -οῦ, ὁ	1) compatriot; neighbor; 2) brothers and sisters
αἰώνιος, -ον	1) long ages ago; 2) eternal; 3) permanent, lasting
ἀλλήλων, -οις, -ους [19]	each other, one another, mutually
ἄν	"a multivalent marker that nuances verbs with an aspect of contingency or generalization"; would, ever, might
ἀπεκρίθη	he/she/it answered (3rd pers. sg. aor. ἀποκρίνομαι)
δοῦλος, -ου, ὁ	slave
ἐάν	if
ἔξω	adv. outside; a) out(side), prep. w. gen. out (of/from); b) w. art. those outside, outsiders
εἰ μή	(if not); except, unless
ἐκκλησία, -ας, ἡ	1) assembly; 2) assembly, congregation
ἐμός, ἐμή, ἐμόν	1st pers. poss. pron. my, mine
ἐντολή, -ῆς, ἡ	commandment, order, instruction
ἐπί [ἐπ', ἐφ']	prep. 1a) w. gen. on, over, at, before, in the presence of, on the basis of; 1b) w. dat. on, over, at, because of, on top of, in addition to, to, on the basis of, near, in regard to, about, along the lines of, for, against; 1c) w. acc. over, upon, on, against, up to, to, at, toward, in addition to, to, for; 2a) w. gen. in/at the time of, In the course of, at; 2b) w. dat. at the time of, at, on, over a period of, for; 3) w. dat. in
ἡμεῖς	we (nom. pl. ἐγώ)
θέλημα, -ματος, τό	1) will; 2) will, desire
ἰδέ; ἰδού	(you) see!; behold, look, see (impv. ὁράω/ εἶδον)
κακός, -ή, -όν	1) bad, something bad, a wrong; 2) harmful, bad
καλός, -ή, -όν	fine, good
καθώς	a) as, just as; b) to the extent/degree that; c) inasmuch as, since

---

[19] The first form is the genitive (of the reciprocal pronoun), second the dative, and third the accusative. Its number and gender cannot be known apart from the noun/pronoun it depends on.

μήτηρ, μητρός, ἡ	mother
μοῦ	my (gen. ἐγώ)
νεκρός, -ά, -όν	dead one, corpse
οὐδέ	a) no; b) neither, nor; c) not even, not; d-e) not even
οὐδείς, οὐδεμία, οὐδέν	a) adj. no; b) n. no one, nobody, nothing, not a thing, in no way, not (be) worth consideration, amount to nothing
παραβολή, -ῆς, ἡ	a) illustration, parable; b) symbol
πιστός, -ή, -όν	1) reliable, faithful, truthworthy; 2) believing (with commitment), n. believer
πονηρός, -ά, -όν	1) bad, envious; 2) bad, poor; 3) bad, virulent
πρῶτος, -η, -ον	1) first, earlier, earliest, outer (part); 2) first, most prominent/important, first (of all)
τρίτος, -η, -ον	1) third; 2) third part
ὑμεῖς	you (all) (nom. pl. σύ)
ὧδε	adv. a) here, to this place, hither; b) here, in this place, in this connection

5 Personal Pronouns

5.1 Introduction

5.1.1 *Pronouns* are words that take the place of nouns. Example: "She stopped talking" or "it looked green." Pronouns designate an object that can be known from the context or usage, or because it has already been mentioned.

5.1.2 The word that a pronoun substitutes or refers to is called the *antecedent*.

5.1.3 Pronouns can do more than simply substitute for nouns. They can also clarify (make clear) and connotate (emphasize or contrast).[1]

5.1.4 There are different types of pronouns. The three most common types in the New Testament are *personal pronouns* (10,779), *demonstrative pronouns* (1,651), and *relative pronouns* (1,551). This chapter will focus on personal pronouns, and the next chapter will focus on demonstrative and relative pronouns. But before going on to any of these, we should look at a few general observations about pronouns.

5.2 The Grammar of Pronouns

5.2.1 The case of a pronoun is determined by its function in the sentence (just like a regular noun).

5.2.2 The gender and number of a pronoun is determined by its *antecedent*. For example, in the sentence "Lindsey is upset, and she doesn't want to talk to anyone" the word "Lindsey" is the antecedent of the pronoun "she."

---

[1] See "The Three Uses of αὐτός" below.

5.2.3   Just like English, Greek has first, second and third person pronouns, which designates the person speaking, the person being spoken to, and the person being spoken about.

5.2.3.1   1st person pronoun: I = ἐγώ

5.2.3.2   2nd person pronoun: You = σύ

5.2.3.3   3rd person pronoun: He, she, or it = αὐτός, -ή, -ό

5.3   First and Second Person Pronouns

5.3.1   First and second person pronouns refer to the person speaking (1st) and the person being spoken to (2nd).

5.3.2   Since first and second person pronouns are indeclinable, they have no gender. However, since personal pronouns refer to persons, it is often necessary to know the *biological* gender of the pronoun (e.g., is ὑμᾶς, "you," speaking of a group of men or women, or both?). Biological gender (sex), along with number, can usually (though not always) be known by the pronoun's antecedent and the context of the verse.[2]

1st Person		2nd Person	
ἐγώ	I	σύ	you
μου (ἐμοῦ)	my	σου (σοῦ)	your
μοι (ἐμοί)	to me	σοι (σοί)	to you
με (ἐμέ)	me	σε (σέ)	you
ἡμεῖς	we	ὑμεῖς	you (all)
ἡμῶν	our	ὑμῶν	your
ἡμῖν	to us	ὑμῖν	to you (all)
ἡμᾶς	us	ὑμᾶς	you (all)

5.3.3   As you can see, first and second person pronouns closely follow the third declension section of the *Table of Case Endings*.

---

[2] Who are the "they" who "spoke the word of God with boldness" in Acts 4:31? Trace the antecedent "they" as far back as you can in the book of Acts to find out which genders are included in this group. (Hint: Lk 24:10, 22; Acts 1:14; 2:17-18; and 5:1, 14).

5.3.4 The genitive forms of pronouns usually come after the word they modify. Example: Μεγαλύνει ἡ ψυχή μου τὸν κύριον is translated "my soul exalts the Lord."³

5.3.5 In contemporary English,⁴ there is unfortunately no second-person plural personal pronoun.⁵ "You" can mean either "you" (a person) or "you" (a group of people). Therefore, translating ὑμεῖς, ὑμῶν, ὑμῖν, and ὑμᾶς may require adding the word "all" for precision.⁶

1ˢᵗ	2ⁿᵈ	3ʳᵈ M	3ʳᵈ F	3ʳᵈ N
ἐγώ	σύ	αὐτός	αὐτή	αὐτό
μου (ἐμοῦ)	σου (σοῦ)	αὐτοῦ	αὐτῆς	αὐτοῦ
μοι (ἐμοί)	σοι (σοί)	αὐτῷ	αὐτῇ	αὐτῷ
με (ἐμέ)	σε (σέ)	αὐτόν	αὐτήν	αὐτό
ἡμεῖς	ὑμεῖς	αὐτοί	αὐταί	αὐτά
ἡμῶν	ὑμῶν	αὐτῶν	αὐτῶν	αὐτῶν
ἡμῖν	ὑμῖν	αὐτοῖς	αὐταῖς	αὐτοῖς
ἡμᾶς	ὑμᾶς	αὐτούς	αὐτάς	αὐτά

Τοσούτῳ χρόνῳ μεθ' ὑμῶν εἰμι καὶ οὐκ ἔγνωκάς με, Φίλιππε; ὁ ἑωρακὼς ἐμὲ ἑώρακεν τὸν πατέρα· πῶς σὺ λέγεις, Δεῖξον ἡμῖν τὸν πατέρα;

---

³ Lk 1:46.
⁴ The two exceptions include (1) Middle-English ("ye") and (2) the Southern colloquialism "ya'll" (a contraction of "you all"). I discuss this more in chapter 17.
⁵ The same goes for Hebrew, which can be significant (e.g., "you" in Gen 3:1-5). See chapter 17.
⁶ In some cases, translations provide a footnote denoting the plural.

"Have I been with <u>you</u> all this time, Philip, and <u>you</u> still do not know <u>me</u>? Whoever has seen <u>me</u> has seen the Father. How can <u>you</u> say, 'Show <u>us</u> the Father'?"[7]

5.4 Third Person Pronoun

5.4.1 The third person pronoun in Greek is the 2-1-2 word αὐτός. Unlike first and second person pronouns, αὐτός is declinable, so it has the aspect of gender. The gender and number of the pronoun is determined by its antecedent in the sentence.

5.4.2 There are three major functions of αὐτός: *Personal Pronoun, Adjectival Intensive,* and *Identical Adjective*:

5.4.2.1 **Personal Pronoun** — This is the most common and natural use of αὐτός. Context determines if αὐτός is being used as a personal pronoun.

ἄρα γε ἀπὸ τῶν καρπῶν <u>αὐτῶν</u> ἐπιγνώσεσθε <u>αὐτούς</u>
"Thus you will know <u>them</u> by <u>their</u> fruits."[8]

καὶ προσελθόντες οἱ μαθηταὶ <u>αὐτοῦ</u> ἠρώτουν <u>αὐτὸν</u> λέγοντες, Ἀπόλυσον <u>αὐτήν</u>, ὅτι κράζει ὄπισθεν ἡμῶν.[9]

And <u>his</u> disciples came and urged <u>him</u>, saying, "Send <u>her</u> away, for <u>she</u> keeps shouting at us."[10]

ὁ δὲ εἶπεν πρὸς <u>αὐτούς</u>, Μηδὲν πλέον παρὰ τὸ διατεταγμένον <u>ὑμῖν</u> πράσσετε.
He said to <u>them</u>, "Collect no more than the amount prescribed for <u>you</u>."[11]

---

[7] Jn 14:9.
[8] Mt 7:20.
[9] "ἡμῶν" at the end of this verse is likely functioning as an objective genitive. See 2.7.1.10.
[10] Mt 15:23.
[11] Lk 3:13.

5.4.2.2 **Adjectival Intensive** — This function gives emphasis to the antecedent instead of replacing it. αὐτός will often[12] be in the predicate position[13] if it is functioning as an adjectival intensive.

αὐτὸς γὰρ ὁ πατὴρ φιλεῖ ὑμᾶς.
for the father <u>himself</u> loves you.[14]

...καὶ ὑπὸ <u>αὐτῆς</u> τῆς ἀληθείας.
...and so has the truth <u>itself</u>.[15]

καὶ <u>αὐτοὶ</u> οὐκ εἰσῆλθον εἰς τὸ πραιτώριον.
They <u>themselves</u> did not enter the headquarters.[16]

5.4.2.3 **Identical Adjective** — This function is used as an identical adjective which means "same." αὐτός will often be in the attributive position[17] if it's an identical adjective.

Διαιρέσεις δὲ χαρισμάτων εἰσίν, τὸ δὲ <u>αὐτὸ</u> πνεῦμα· καὶ διαιρέσεις διακονιῶν εἰσιν, καὶ ὁ <u>αὐτὸς</u> κύριος· καὶ διαιρέσεις ἐνεργημάτων εἰσίν, ὁ δὲ <u>αὐτὸς</u> θεός,

Now there are varieties of gifts, but the <u>same</u> Spirit; and there are varieties of services, but the <u>same</u> Lord; and there are varieties of activities, but it is the <u>same</u> God.[18]

... προσηύξατο ἐκ τρίτου τὸν <u>αὐτὸν</u> λόγον εἰπὼν πάλιν.
... and prayed for the third time saying the <u>same</u> words [again].[19]

---

[12] In contrast with Wallace, *GGBB*, 348-349, Mounce in *BBG*, 102-3 notes the significant number of exceptions with regard to the predicate/attributive position of the adjectival intensive and identitical adjective functions of the third person pronoun.
[13] Predicate position means the article comes before the noun, but not before the adjective/pronoun.
[14] Jn 16:27.
[15] 3 Jn 1:12.
[16] Jn 18:28.
[17] Attributive position means the article comes before the adjective/pronoun.
[18] 1 Cor 12:4-6.

5.4.3   *Table of Personal Pronouns*

1ˢᵗ	2ⁿᵈ	3ʳᵈ M	3ʳᵈ F	3ʳᵈ N
ἐγώ	σύ	αὐτός	αὐτή	αὐτό
μου (ἐμοῦ)	σου (σοῦ)	αὐτοῦ	αὐτῆς	αὐτοῦ
μοι (ἐμοί)	σοι (σοί)	αὐτῷ	αὐτῇ	αὐτῷ
με (ἐμέ)	σε (σέ)	αὐτόν	αὐτήν	αὐτό
ἡμεῖς	ὑμεῖς	αὐτοί	αὐταί	αυτά
ἡμῶν	ὑμῶν	αὐτῶν	αὐτῶν	αὐτῶν
ἡμῖν	ὑμῖν	αὐτοῖς	αὐταῖς	αὐτοῖς
ἡμᾶς	ὑμᾶς	αὐτούς	αὐτάς	αὐτά

5.4.4   As you may have noticed, αὐτός looks almost exactly like the *Table of Articles* but with αυ added in the front. So if you know the forms of the article, you know all the forms of αὐτός.

1ˢᵗ	2ⁿᵈ	3ʳᵈ M	3ʳᵈ F	3ʳᵈ N
ἐγώ	σύ	αὐτός	αὐτή	αὐτό
μου (ἐμοῦ)	σου (σοῦ)	αὐτοῦ	αὐτῆς	αὐτοῦ
μοι (ἐμοί)	σοι (σοί)	αὐτῷ	αὐτῇ	αὐτῷ
με (ἐμέ)	σε (σέ)	αὐτόν	αὐτήν	αὐτό
ἡμεῖς	ὑμεῖς	αὐτοί	αὐταί	αυτά
ἡμῶν	ὑμῶν	αὐτῶν	αὐτῶν	αὐτῶν
ἡμῖν	ὑμῖν	αὐτοῖς	αὐταῖς	αὐτοῖς
ἡμᾶς	ὑμᾶς	αὐτούς	αὐτάς	αὐτά

καὶ ἔδησεν <u>αὐτὸν</u> ἐν φυλακῇ διὰ Ἡρῳδιάδα τὴν γυναῖκα Φιλίππου τοῦ ἀδελφοῦ <u>αὐτοῦ</u>, ὅτι <u>αὐτὴν</u> ἐγάμησεν·

---

[19] Mt 26:44. It is odd that the NRSV, KJV, and NIV do not translate πάλιν.

"...bound him, and put him in prison on account of Herodias, his brother Philip's wife, because Herod had married her."[20]

Vocabulary

αἰών, -ῶνος, ὁ	1) in the past, ages ago, eternity; 2) age; 3) world; 4) Aeon
γυνή, γυναικός, ἡ	1) woman; 2) wife
διδάσκαλος, -ου, ὁ	teacher, instructor
δικαιοσύνη, -ης, ἡ	uprightness, righteousness, justice
δώδεκα	twelve
ἑαυτοῦ, -ῆς, -οῦ	reflex. pron. 1) self/selves; 2) each other, one another; 3) poss. pron. his, her, their
ἐκεῖνος, -η, -ο	dem. pron. that (person/thing) (pl. those)
ἐλπίς, -ίδος, ἡ	1) hope, expectation; 2-3) hope
εὐθύς	adv. immediately, at once
ἕως	1) till, until, as long as, while; 2) as far as, to, until, (up) to, until
ἤ	1) or, either...or; 2) than, rather; before
κἀγώ	and I; (and) I too/also/in turn, On my part, I on the other hand, as for me
μαθητής, -ου, ὁ	a) pupil; b) adherent, disciple
μακάριος, -ια, -ιον	blessed, privileged, fortunate, happy
μέγας, μεγάλη, μέγα and μείζων, -ον	great, greater, very exceptional, outstanding
μέν	a) on the one hand/indeed/now...but, one...another, some...others, at times...at other times; b) now, so then, rather
μηδείς, μηδεμία, μηδέν	1) adj. no, (not) any; 2) n. nobody, nothing, anything, not...at all, in no way, without...at all
μόνος, -η, -ον	a) adj. alone, only; b) adv. merely, just, only
ὅπως	1) adv. how, that; 2) conj. (in order) that, as to how
ὅσος, -η, -ον	1) as much as, as long as; 2) as many (much) as, all who, whatever/everything that; 3) to the degree/extent that
οὖν	ppos. a) so, then, hence; b) then, now, so, in turn

---

[20] Mk 6:17. Note how the NRSV (and NET) uses the antecedent ("Herod") instead of "he" (KJV, ESV, NASB) for clarity in the last phrase.

οφθαλμός, -οῦ, ὁ	eye, sight
πάλιν	adv. a) again, once more, on the other hand, in turn, what's more, moreoever; b) back
πόλις, -εως, ἡ	a) city, town; b) inhabitants
πολύς, πολλή, πολυ, or πλείων, πλεῖον, πλέον	a) adj. pl. many; b) adj. much, great, long, greater, still more, longer, many, most, large, big, immense, vast; c) n. many things, much, adv. greatly, many, the many, most
πούς, ποδός, ὁ	foot
πῶς	adv. 1) how?, in what manner/way?, how is it then?, how can it be that?, by what right?, in what sense?; 2) how!
σημεῖον, -ου, τό	sign

6 Demonstrative and Relative Pronouns

6.1 Demonstrative Pronouns

6.1.1 Demonstrative pronouns can function as both pronouns and as adjectives in order to demonstrate or single out an object.

6.1.2 The two most common demonstrative pronouns are οὗτος, αὕτη, τοῦτο (this, these) and ἐκεῖνος, ἐκείνη, ἐκεῖνο (that, those).[1] The former are called *proximal* demonstrative pronouns because they demonstrate something in close proximity (this, these). The latter are called *distal* demonstrative pronouns because they demonstrate something in a distance (that, those).

6.1.3 Demonstrative pronouns follow the standard noun case endings.

6.1.4 *Table of Proximal Demonstrative Pronouns*

M (2)	F (1)	N (2)
οὗτος	αὕτη	τοῦτο
τούτου	ταύτης	τούτου
τούτῳ	ταύτῃ	τούτῳ
τοῦτον	ταύτην	τοῦτο
οὗτοι	αὗται	ταῦτα
τούτων	τούτων	τούτων
τούτοις	ταύταις	τούτοις
τούτους	ταύτας	ταῦτα

---

[1] The third demonstrative pronoun, ὅδε, ἥδε, τόδε, is a rare (10 NT occurrences) contraction of the Greek articles ὁ ἡ τό and δέ, sometimes meaning "this" or "here."

6.1.5 Table of Distal Demonstrative Pronouns

M (2)	F (1)	N (2)
ἐκεῖνος	ἐκείνη	ἐκεῖνο
ἐκείνου	ἐκείνης	ἐκείνου
ἐκείνῳ	ἐκείνῃ	ἐκείνῳ
ἐκεῖνον	ἐκείνην	ἐκεῖνο
ἐκεῖνοι	ἐκεῖναι	ἐκεῖνα
ἐκείνων	ἐκείνων	ἐκείνων
ἐκείνοις	ἐκείναις	ἐκείνοις
ἐκείνους	ἐκείνας	ἐκεῖνα

ἐν τούτῳ γινώσκομεν ὅτι ἀγαπῶμεν τὰ τέκνα τοῦ θεοῦ.
By this we know that we love the children of God.[2]

Ἀπόλυσον τοὺς ἀνθρώπους ἐκείνους.
Let those men go.[3]

...αὗται γάρ εἰσιν δύο διαθῆκαι.
...; these women are two covenants.[4]

διδάσκαλε, αὕτη ἡ γυνὴ κατείληπται ἐπ' αὐτοφώρῳ μοιχευομένη·
Teacher, this woman has been caught in adultery, in the very act.[5]

6.1.6 When functioning as *pronouns*, the case of a demonstrative pronoun is determined by its function in the sentence and its

---

[2] 1 Jn 5:2.
[3] Acts 16:35.
[4] Gal 4:24. Notice how translations like the NRSV, CEB and NIV render γάρ by the use of an English colon, while the NASB and NET do not.
[5] Jn 8:4.

Chapter Six: Demonstrative and Relative Pronouns

gender and number are determined by its antecedent (just like a normal pronoun).

6.1.7 When functioning as *adjectives*, the case, number, and gender are determined by the noun it is modifying (just like a normal adjective). However, the positions of the articles in the function of demonstrative adjectives are the exact opposite of normal adjectives. With normal adjectives, if there is an article before the noun, the adjective functions *predicately*. But with demonstrative adjectives, if there is an article before the noun, the demonstrative adjective functions *attributively*. Why is the grammar this way? It is because demonstrative adjectives function attributively and are always in the predicate position. Example: ὁ δοῦλος οὗτος and οὗτος ὁ δοῦλος means "this servant."

6.2 Relative Pronoun

6.2.1 Relative pronouns *relate* to more than one clause. They refer back to an antecedent in the previous clause and also function in some way in their own clause.

6.2.1.1 Example: "Fred is a rancher, who sold his cattle this month."

"Who" is the relative pronoun, "Fred" is the antecendent, and "who sold his cattle this month" is the relative clause.

6.2.2 Like αὐτός, the number and gender of a relative pronoun (usually) matches the antecedent. The case of the relative pronoun is determined by its function in the relative clause.

6.2.3 The two relative pronouns in Greek are the definite relative pronoun ὅς, ἥ, ὅ ("who," "whom," "that," "which," "whose") and the indefinite relative pronoun ὅστις, ἥστις, ὅτι ("who," "which").[6]

6.2.3.1 ὅς, ἥ, ὅ is the *definite* relative pronoun, which describes, clarifies, or restricts the meaning of the noun. It is the most common relative pronoun.

---

[6] As noted in *CL,* 257, the indefinite relative pronoun is a combination of the definite relative pronoun (ὅς) and the enclitic indefinite pronoun (τις, τι).

6.2.3.2 *Table of Definite Relative Pronouns*

M	F	N	gloss
ὅς	ἥ	ὅ	who/which/that
οὗ	ἧς	οὗ	of whom/which
ᾧ	ᾗ	ᾧ	to whom/which
ὅν	ἥν	ὅ	whom/which/that
οἵ	αἵ	ἅ	who/which/that
ὧν	ὧν	ὧν	of whom/which
οἷς	αἷς	οἷς	to whom/which
οὕς	ἅς	ἅ	whom/which/that

6.2.3.2.1 Notice (below) how similar the relative pronoun paradigm is to the *Table of Articles*. The relative pronoun is basically the article without the tau.

Article			Relative Pronoun		
M	F	N	M	F	N
ὁ	ἡ	τό	ὅς	ἥ	ὅ
τοῦ	τῆς	τοῦ	οὗ	ἧς	οὗ
τῷ	τῇ	τῷ	ᾧ	ᾗ	ᾧ
τόν	τήν	τό	ὅν	ἥν	ὅ
οἱ	αἱ	τά	οἵ	αἵ	ἅ
τῶν	τῶν	τῶν	ὧν	ὧν	ὧν
τοῖς	ταῖς	τοῖς	οἷς	αἷς	οἷς
τούς	τάς	τά	οὕς	ἅς	ἅ

6.2.3.2.2   As you can see, the key to identifying the definite relative pronoun is to look for the rough breathing mark.

6.2.3.3   ὅστις, ἥτις, ὅτι is the *indefinite* relative pronoun and is either *generic* or *qualitative*.

6.2.3.3.1   If being used *generically*, ὅστις focuses on the whole class of persons ("who") or things ("which"). Thus, "whoever" = "everyone who," and "whichever" = "everything which." Example:

ἀλλ' ὅστις σε ῥαπίζει εἰς τὴν δεξιὰν σιαγόνα [σου], στρέψον αὐτῷ καὶ τὴν ἄλλην·
But if <u>anyone</u> strikes you on the right cheek, turn the other also.[7]

6.2.3.3.2   If being used *qualitatively* (or "essentially"), ὅστις focuses on the quality or essence of the person ("who") or thing ("which"). Example:

ἀσπάσασθε Μαρίαν, ἥτις πολλὰ ἐκοπίασεν εἰς ὑμᾶς.
Greet Mary, <u>who</u> has worked very hard among you.[8]

6.2.4   Relative pronouns typically occur in a relative clause. The relative clause is always dependent, which means it will not contain the main subject nor the verb of a sentence.[9] Examples:

ἐξ ἧς ἐγεννήθη Ἰησοῦς ὁ λεγόμενος Χριστός.
...<u>of whom</u> Jesus was born, who is called the Messiah.[10]

...σωτῆρος ἡμῶν θεοῦ, ὃς πάντας ἀνθρώπους θέλει σωθῆναι.
...God our Savior, <u>who</u> desires everyone to be saved.[11]

---

[7] Mt 5:39.
[8] Rom 16:6.
[9] Note that in the absence of an immediate antecedent, it is possible to supply a pronoun as needed. This makes translation smoother.
[10] Mt 1:16.
[11] 1 Tm 2:3b-4.

M	F	N
ὅς	ἥ	ὅ
οὗ	ἧς	οὗ
ᾧ	ᾗ	ᾧ
ὅν	ἥν	ὅ
οἵ	αἵ	ἅ
ὧν	ὧν	ὧν
οἷς	αἷς	οἷς
οὕς	ἅς	ἅ

Ἀφορίσατε δή μοι τὸν Βαρναβᾶν καὶ Σαῦλον εἰς τὸ ἔργον ὃ προσκέκλημαι αὐτούς.

"Set apart for me Barnabas and Saul for the work to <u>which</u> I have called them.[12]

παντὶ δὲ ᾧ ἐδόθη πολύ, πολὺ ζητηθήσεται παρ' αὐτοῦ...

From everyone <u>to whom</u> much has been given, much will be required...[13]

μακάριος ὁ δοῦλος ἐκεῖνος ὃν ἐλθὼν
ὁ κύριος αὐτοῦ εὑρήσει οὕτως
ποιοῦντα·

Blessed is that slave <u>whom</u> his master will find at work when he arrives.[14]

M	F	N
ὅς	ἥ	ὅ
οὗ	ἧς	οὗ
ᾧ	ᾗ	ᾧ
ὅν	ἥν	ὅ
οἵ	αἵ	ἅ
ὧν	ὧν	ὧν
οἷς	αἷς	οἷς
οὕς	ἅς	ἅ

---

[12] Acts 13:2.
[13] Lk 12:48. Notice that the NRSV's priority of gender-inclusiveness results in a non-rendering of αὐτοῦ ("required *of him*"), though this does not negatively effect the meaning of the text.
[14] Mt 26:46.

Chapter Six: Demonstrative and Relative Pronouns

Vocabulary

ἀλήθεια, -ας, ἡ	truth
εἰρήνη, -ης, ἡ	1-2) peace
ἐνώπιον	prep. w. gen. a) ahead; b) in presence (of); c) in front (of); d) before, under, scrutiny, in sight (of); e) before
ἐπαγγελία, -ας, ἡ	promise
ἑπτά	seven
θρόνος, -ου, ὁ	throne, the enthroned
Ἰερουσαλήμ, ἡ or Ἰερουσαλήμα, τά/ἡ	Jerusalem
κεφαλή, -ῆς, ἡ	head
ὁδός, -οῦ, ἡ	1) way, road, highway, path; 2) way, journey, trip, the Way
ὅς, ἥ, ὅ	who, which/what, that
ὅτε	when, as long as, while
οὕτω/οὕτως	in this way/manner/fashion
πλοῖον, -ου, τό	ship, boat
ῥῆμα, -ματος, τό	1) statement, pronouncement, declaration; 2) a matter, thing, event
χείρ, χειρός, ἡ	1-2) hand
ψυχή, -ῆς, ἡ	1) life; 2) person, creature; 3) life, (inner) self, soul

7 Introduction to Verbs and Present Active Indicative

7.1 Introduction to Verbs

7.1.1 Verbs are like articles, adjectives, and pronouns in that they have to *agree* with what they are modifying, what they are related to, or what they are replacing. Example: "I were" is incorrect English. It should be "I was." The number (singular, plural) and tense (present, past, etc.) along with other properties determine what the verb looks like. Those "other properties" are the focus of this section.

7.1.2 For convenience, we will first begin with properties of verbs that are contained in the *Table of Verb Endings* (see next page).

7.1.2.1 **Person** — Just like English, Greek verbs have three persons: the person speaking (1st), the person being spoken to (2nd), and the person or thing being spoken about (3rd). The verb must agree with its subject in person. In English, we do not say "I were," "They was," or "the dogs jumps over the bush," but rather, "I was," "they were," and "the dogs jump over the bush." Greek makes these distinctions through *personal endings*. Example: if the subject is "we," Greek uses the personal ending "μεν." So, the phrase "if we say" is Ἐὰν εἴπωμεν.[1]

7.1.2.2 **Number** — Just like nouns, verbs are either singular or plural. Personal endings also determine the number.

---
[1] 1 Jn 1:6.

Chapter Seven: Intro to Verbs and Present Active Indicative

7.1.2.3 **Voice** — The Greek also uses personal endings to distinguish between the active, passive, and middle voice.[2]

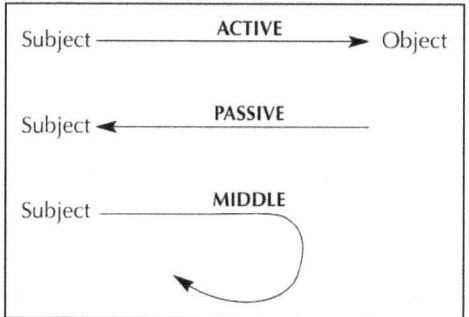

7.1.2.3.1 *Active voice* — the subject performs, produces, or experiences the action. The active emphasizes the *action* of the verb. Example: "I guard."

7.1.2.3.2 *Middle voice* — the subject both does the action and receives the action. The middle emphasizes the *actor* or *subject* of the verb. Example: "I am on my guard." Since there is not always a translational equivalent of the middle voice in English, the middle-voice is often translated as active voice.

7.1.2.3.3 *Passive voice* — the subject receives the action. Example: "I am guarded."

7.1.3 As I said above, all of these three properties are contained in a single *Table of Verb Endings*, which is perhaps the most important table to memorize in learning Greek verbs.

---

[2] The image comes from Wallace, *GGBB*, 409, "Chart 41."

7.2 Table of Verb Endings

		Primary Endings		Secondary Endings	
Active Voice	Singular	λύω		ἔλυον	v/α
		λύεις	ς	ἔλυες	ς
		λύει	ι	ἔλυε(ν)	(ν)
	Plural	λύομεν	μεν	ἐλύομεν	μεν
		λύετε	τε	ἐλύετε	τε
		λύουσι(ν)	σι	ἔλυον	ν
Midd/Pass Voice	Singular	λύομαι	μαι	ἐλυόμην	μην
		λύῃ	σαι	ἐλύου	σο
		λύεται	ται	ἐλύετο	το
	Plural	λυόμεθα	μεθα	ἐλυόμεθα	μεθα
		λύεσθε	σθε	ἐλύεσθε	σθε
		λύονται	νται	ἐλύοντο	ντο

7.2.1 Notes about the *Table of Verb Endings*

7.2.1.1 Each group of three rows is listed in order of person (first, second, third). Example: λυω means "I destroy" while λύεις means "you destroy."[3]

7.2.1.2 The major difference between the primary and secondary endings is that the secondary endings have the augment (ε).[4]

7.2.1.3 Notice that the first person singular in the primary active endings is blank. (Shouldn't it read λυ instead of λυω? No, because the connecting vowel o lengthens to ω.)[5]

---

[3] If it helps, feel free to pencil in the person (1st, 2nd, 3rd) in the table.
[4] The other difference is that the primary endings use present, future, and perfect tenses, while the secondary endings use imperfect, aorist, and pluperfect tenses.
[5] This is similar to how genitive nouns lengthen from o to ω.

7.2.1.4 Notice that the first person singular in the secondary active endings has two options, ν or α. The ending ν is used if it is preceded by a vowel, and α if preceded by a consonant.[6]

7.2.1.5 Because a σ often drops out when standing between two vowels, the endings σαι and σο lose their σ when preceded by an ε.

7.2.1.6 The third plural secondary ending ν can switch to σαν in the aorist passive tense.[7]

7.3 Additional Properties of Greek Verbs

7.3.1 **Mood** — The verbal mood is the "speaker's or writer's *attitude toward the relation of the verbal action to reality*."[8] There are three moods in Greek:

7.3.1.1 *Indicative* mood is the mood of assertion. It is the most common mood. It is used to make a statement of fact or when asking a question. Example: "You are right" or "what are you doing?"

7.3.1.2 *Subjunctive* mood is used to represent the verbal action as uncertain but probable. Example: "You might be right" or "maybe he is busy."

7.3.1.3 *Imperative* mood is the mood of intention and is used to make a command. Example: "Do what's right!" or "Go to work!"

---

[6] See Mounce, *Morphology*, 80.
[7] See 11.6.
[8] Porter, *Fundamentals*, 41.

7.3.2 **Tense, Tense-Stem, Time, and Aspect** — Unlike nouns, verbs loosely inflect the elements of time. But it is important not to confuse the different concepts of tense, tense-stem, time, and aspect.[9]

7.3.2.1 **Tense** — this is the general grammatical category of verbs, which exhibit time (loosely) and aspect (more firmly). Because of that "loose" association, the six Greek tenses (present, imperfect, future, aorist, perfect, pluperfect) do not always correspond to their tense-stems (their morphological form).[10]

7.3.2.2 **Tense Stem/Form** — this is the morphological *form* the verb takes (e.g., present tense-stem, aorist tense-stem, etc.),[11] and usually, but not always corresponds to a verb's tense. Certain tense stems can have more than one dimension of time.

7.3.2.3 **Time** — this is *when* the action of the verb occurs (in the past, present, or future). So there is no such thing as "past *tense*," "present *tense*," or "future *tense*" in Greek; there is only "past time," "present time," and "future time."

7.3.2.4 **Aspect** — this describes *what type of action* took place. This is perhaps the most challenging and controversial area of Greek verbs, but it is important.[12] Generally, there are three aspects in Greek, and each aspect is expressed in certain tenses.

---

[9] There is another property called *Aktionsart*, which (according to Decker, *Reading*, 226), has less to do with how a speaker/writer portrays and experiences the action and more to do with an "objective statement of the *actual nature* of the action/situation." Linguistis often conflate *aktionsart* with verbal aspect, but the overlap is something that continues to be debated.

[10] For example, as you will see in the *Table of Verb Tenses*, the future passive tense uses the aorist passive tense-stem.

[11] This is why many grammarians use the terminology "tense-form." The older terminology is "principle part."

[12] Why challenging and controversial? First of all, grammarians do not all use the same terminology. Second, the names of aspects often conflicts with the the names of tenses (for example the "perfect" tense stem has the "Completive" aspect instead of the "perfect" aspect). Third of all, grammarians do not all agree on what kind of aspect is conveyed through certain tenses. Fourth, different aspects tend to convey different senses of time. Fifth, there is debate about whether aspect is or is not the "primary" dimension of verbs in Greek thought and communication. (Clear as mud?)

Chapter Seven: Intro to Verbs and Present Active Indicative

7.3.2.4.1 *Simple*[13]— views the verbal action as a simple whole. The simple aspect is like a "snapshot" or "summary" of the action. It is expressed in the aorist and future tenses.

7.3.2.4.2 *Continuous*[14] — indicates incompleteness, progress, and process. The continuous aspect usually uses the present and imperfect tenses.

7.3.2.4.3 *Completive*[15] — views the action as brought to completion. It also views the action as having continuous results in the present, or reflects upon a current state of affairs. The completive aspect uses the perfect and pluperfect tenses.

7.3.3 Relating these elements can be confusing. In English we relate all of these elements together without much thought (but that does not make them easier to understand!)[16]

7.3.4 Below is the *Table of Verb Properties*, which connects the relationships between all of these properties:

"Tense"	Tense-Stem	Time	Aspect	Examples
Present	Present	Present	*Continuous*: Action is viewed as being in progress	I am seeing.
Imperfect		Past		I was seeing.
Future	Future Active	Future	*Simple*: Action is viewed as a simple whole, without defining how long the action takes place.	I will see.
Aorist	Aorist Passive	*indicative*: Past (absolute) *participial*: Past (relative)		
	Aorist Active			I saw.
Perfect	Perfect Active	Past	*Completive*: Action is viewed as being brought to completion and is felt at the speaker's present.	I have seen.
Pluperfect	Perfect Passive			I had seen. I had been seeing.

---

[13] Or "Stative."
[14] Or "Imperfective," "Progressive."
[15] Or "Perfective," "Perfect."
[16] Discuss, for example, the differences in meaning between the two sentences: "I could have been having a good time at the pool, but Mom didn't let me;" "I could have had a fun time at the pool, but Mom didn't let me"; "I could have a fun time at the pool, but Mom isn't letting me"; "If I had had a fun time at the pool, Mom would let me."

7.3.5   A few notes about this table:

7.3.5.1   It is important to keep in mind that the contents and organization of this table is academically disputed and simplified. It is adequate enough, however, to communicate the general dimensions of verbs.

7.3.5.2   The two horizontal bold lines underscore the predominance of aspect in Greek verbs and not time. This is one of the biggest differences between English and Greek: *aspect, not time, is more primary to what the grammatical form is conveying*.

7.3.5.3   The dotted lines, likewise, indicate the relativity of time.

7.4   Introduction to Verbal Syntax

7.4.1   There are some important syntactical (sentence-related) features that characterize how verbs function. To keep matters simple, we will use English in the examples below.

7.4.1.1   *The object of verbs may or may not have a substantive* (or object). Verbs with an object are *transitive* (e.g., I drove the car"), and verbs without an object are *intransitive* (e.g., "After the court hearing, I marveled").

7.4.1.2   *The immediate object of a transitive verb may be indirect instead of direct.* Examples:

Indirect object: "She taught him a lesson."
Object complement: "Jack appointed Henry chairman."[17]

7.4.1.3   *Intransitive verbs may not have direct objects, but they can still modify a subject. Predicate nominatives* rename the subject, and *predicate adjectives* describe or modify the subject simply by some version of "is" or "to be." Examples:

Predicate nominative: "Judith was a teacher."
Predicate adjective: "John is heavy-handed sometimes."

---

[17] Here, Henry is the direct object and "chairman" the complement.

Chapter Seven: Intro to Verbs and Present Active Indicative

7.5 The Basic Forms of Greek Verbs

7.5.1 In the end, Greek verbs are words with a few basic components: the verb (tense) stem, the connecting vowel or tense formative, and the personal ending.

$$\boxed{\text{Stem}} + \boxed{\text{CV/TF}} + \boxed{\text{Personal Ending}}$$

7.5.1.1 *Stem* — this is same as "tense stem"; it is the root of a verb in a given tense. The root/stem may both be said to carry the basic meaning of the verb.[18]

7.5.1.2 *Tense Formative/Connecting Vowel*— depending on the tense, Greek adds a letter after a stem to make the pronunciation of a word easier. A tense formative (usually σ) is a consonant, and a connecting vowel is ο or ε.[19]

7.5.1.3 *Personal Endings* — personal endings are suffixes at the end of a verb that reveal the number, person, and voice of a verb.[20]

7.5.2 Example: the word λύομεν (gloss: "we destroy").

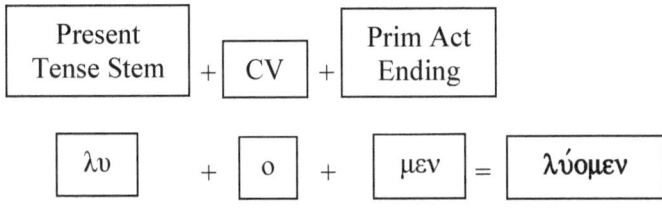

7.5.3 In the indicative mood, if the ending is οι or begins with a μ or a ν, the connecting vowel is ο. In every other case the connecting vowel is ε. If there is no ending, the connecting vowel can be either ο or ε.

---

[18] Recall that nouns, verbs, and adjectives can share the same root, but not the same stem. Refer to 2.1-2.2 on the meaning of "roots" and "stems."
[19] As you will learn, the future tense is the only tense to use both the connecting vowel and the tense formative. The perfect middle passive and the pluperfect middle/passive are the only tenses that don't use either.
[20] "CV" = Connecting Vowel. "TF" = Tense Formative.

7.6 Present Active Indicative

7.6.1 The Present Active Indicative is an action that occurs in the speaker's present time ("present indicative") where the subject performs, produces, or experiences the action ("active"). It usually has the continuous aspect, though it can at times express a simple aspect.[21] Example: "I am guarding."

7.6.2 *Table of Verb Tenses*

Tense	Aug/ Red	Tense stem	TF + CV	Endings	First singular
Pres act		pres	o/ε	prim act	λύω
Pres mid/pas		pres	o/ε	prim mid/pas	λύομαι

7.6.3 Verbal Form of Present Active Indicative[22]

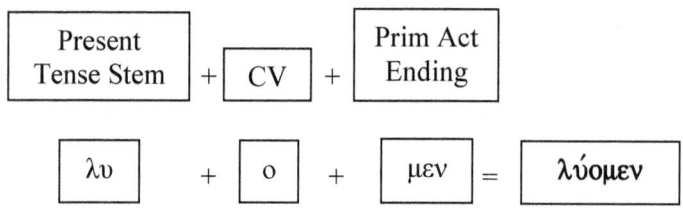

---

[21] See Wallace, *GGBB*, 514; Porter, *Fundamentals*, 84.
[22] This example uses a plural instead of a singular because the singular does't have an ending (see *Table of Verb Tenses*) and therefore makes for a poor example.

Chapter Seven: Intro to Verbs and Present Active Indicative

7.6.4 *Table of Verb Endings*

		Primary Endings		Secondary Endings	
Active Voice	Singular	λύω		ἔλυον	ν/α
		λύεις	ς	ἔλυες	ς
		λύει	ι	ἔλυε(ν)	(ν)
	Plural	λύομεν	μεν	ἐλύομεν	μεν
		λύετε	τε	ἐλύετε	τε
		λύουσι(ν)	σι	ἔλυον	ν
Mid/Pass Voice	Singular	λύομαι	μαι	ἐλυόμην	μην
		λύῃ	σαι	ἐλύου	σο
		λύεται	ται	ἐλύετο	το
	Plural	λυόμεθα	μεθα	ἐλυόμεθα	μεθα
		λύεσθε	σθε	ἐλύεσθε	σθε
		λύονται	νται	ἐλύοντο	ντο

7.6.5 **Paradigm of Present Active Indicative**

	Form	Gloss	CV	Ending
1st Sg	λύω[23]	I am releasing	ο	
2nd Sg	λύεις	You are releasing	ε	ς
3rd Sg	λύει	He/she/it is releasing	ε	ι
1st Pl	λύομεν	We are releasing	ο	μεν
2nd Pl	λύετε	You are releasing	ε	τε
3rd Pl	λύουσι(ν)[24]	They are releasing	ο	σι

---

[23] Note the lengthening of the omicron: ο at the end of word = ω.
[24] Note the contraction and lengthening of the omicron: ο + ο = ου.

7.6.6 Rules on Present Active Indicative

7.6.6.1 Since Greek verbs can tell you the person, when a personal pronoun is used with the verb, it is often used for emphasis. Example: ἀκούω means "I am hearing" while ἐγώ ἀκούω just adds emphasis; "*I* am hearing."[25]

Examples:

Ἀμὴν ἀμὴν <u>λέγω</u> σοι.
Verily, Verily, <u>I am saying</u> to you.[26]

τί δὲ <u>βλέπεις</u> τὸ κάρφος τὸ ἐν τῷ ὀφθαλμῷ τοῦ ἀδελφοῦ σου...
Why do <u>you look</u> at the speck that is in your brother's eye...[27]

7.6.7 Examples from English to Greek

We are <u>guarding</u> the law of love.
<u>Τηροῦμεν</u> τόν νομόν τού ἀγαπου.

His law <u>is guarding</u> us in joy.
Ὁ νόμος ἀυτοῦ <u>τηρεῖ</u> ἡμᾶς ἐν χαρῃ.

Where are demons not <u>speaking</u>?
ὅπου τά δαιμόνια οὐκ <u>λαλοῦσιν</u>;

---

[25] See chapter 17 for more on this topic.
[26] Jn 3:3.
[27] Mt 8:3.

Chapter Seven: Intro to Verbs and Present Active Indicative

Vocabulary

ἀγαπάω	1) love, cherish
ἀκούω	1) hear; 2) understand; 3) hear, hear about, pass. be said/rumored; 4) hear
βλέπω	1) be able to see; 2) see, look at, observe, watch, look on; 3) see, perceive, beware, be on guard (against), look out (for), heed; 4) look/face toward
δαιμόνιον, -ου, τό	1) diety, divine being; 2) hostile/evil spirit, demon
ἔχω	1) have; 2) have (on), wear; 3) have wherewithal, be able; 4) consider, hold (to be), view; 5) have/be, be located, be near, be next, have to do with, relate to
ζητέω	1) seek, look for; 2) deliberate, discuss; 3) desire, seek; 4) expect, demand
καλέω	1) say, call, call (for), summon; 2) call, invite; 3) call
λαλέω	1) to sound, 2) speak (about), talk (about), tell, say, utter
λύω	1) loose, release, allow; 2) abolish; 3) break; 4) demolish, destroy
νόμος, -ου, ὁ	1) custom, norm, principle; 2) law
ὅπου	adv. 1) where, wherever; 2) whereas
οἶδα	1) know; 2) perceive, understand
ὅταν	a) whenever; b) when
πιστεύω	1) believe, give credence (to, about), have faith, be confident, put trust in, pl. n. believers; 2) entrust
πληρόω	1) fill; 2) complete, fulfill, fill (up), carry out
ποιέω	1) make, create, construct; 2) do, perform, make, cause to be, do with, claim, prepare, give, gain, celebrate, hold, exercise, evaluate, consider, show, spend, work
πρόσωπον, -ου, τό	face, countenance, appearance
τηρέω	1) keep, have on hand, watch, put/keep under guard; 2) keep, observe
τότε	temp. adv. a) then; b) at that time, then, thereupon
τυφλός, -ή, όν	1-2) blind
χαρά, -ᾶς, ἡ	1-2) joy

8 Present Middle/Passive Indicative and Contract Verbs

8.1 The Challenge of the Middle Voice

8.1.1 The middle voice is where the subject both does the action and receives the action. To put it differently, the "active voice emphasizes the *action* of the verb; the middle emphasizes the *actor* [subject]."[1]

8.1.2 Here are some examples of what the middle voice might look like in English:

"I take" (active)   "I choose, prefer" (middle)

"I remind" (active)   "I remember" (middle)

"I have" (active)   "I cling to" (middle)

8.1.3 Since there is no middle voice in English, it is often very hard (even impossible) to capture its meaning when translating.

8.1.4 Another problem is that not all verbs can be rendered in all three voices. This is because the meaning of some verbs just can't be rendered in certain voices. This is true in English. For example, how would you say "I go" in the passive voice? "I was go'd"? "Someone go'd me"? It doesn't work. There is no passive meaning (or form) of "I go" in English. Greek has that same problem. Due to the meaning of certain verbs, the *majority* (about 75%) of present middle and imperfect middle indicative verbs[2] in the New Testament don't have an active form, so when they appear in their lexical form they have the middle/passive

---

[1] Wallace, *GGBB*, 415.
[2] Only present tense and imperfect tense verbs have this problem. This is why the present and imperfect tenses combine middle and passive voice in the *Table of Verb Tenses*.

Chapter Eight: Present Middle/Passive Indicative and Contract Verbs

endings.³ A common example is ἔρχομαι. You would think that the lexical form would be ἔρχω since the lexical form is always first person active voice, but it isn't. There is no active form of this word.

8.1.5 The three basic facts about these kinds of verbs is that (1) they usually have the middle/passive ending (μαι) in their lexical form, (2) they are never passive in meaning, and (3) they may or may not be active in meaning.

8.1.6 This last point ("may or may not be active in meaning") is highly disputed by grammarians. There are three popular solutions to this problem: (1) affirm the active meaning of these verbs, (2) reject the active meaning of these verbs, and (3) both affirm and reject the active meaning of these verbs. Below is a brief explanation of each position:

8.1.6.1 First, some grammarians think that we should refer to these verbs as *deponent*, which are always passive in form but active in meaning (Mounce).⁴

8.1.6.2 Second, some swing in the opposite direction and say that "every verb expresses the meaning of its voice form, even when other forms—such as the active voice—may not exist" (Porter).⁵ Therefore, the entire category of "deponency" should be rejected.

8.1.6.3 Third, some argue that that *some* of these verbs are truly "deponent" (are active in meaning and middle/passive in form) and some are not. Wallace advocates this position and argues that "A deponent middle verb is one that has no active form for a particular *principal part*⁶ in *Hellenistic* Greek, *and* one whose force in that principal part is evidently active. Thus, for example, ἔρχομαι has no active form for the first principal part,

---

³ Lexicons don't always agree, however. Compare πορεύομαι (Louw and Nida) to πορεύω (Danker), both of which reflect the same word. Wisely, Swanson's *DBL* lists both (4513).
⁴ Mounce, *BBG*, 154.
⁵ Porter, *Fundamentals*, 125.
⁶ I.e., verb root.

but it is obviously active in force."[7] On the other hand, "There are some verbs that never had an active form, yet the true middle force is clearly seen. For example, δέχομαι means I receive, I welcome—an idea that is inherently reflexive."[8] Wallace then goes on to provide a list of "truly deponent verbs" and those that only *appear* to be deponent.

8.1.7 If Wallace's approach is the most accurate (and I think it is), then most of the time it is safe to think of "deponent" verbs as middle/passive in form and active in meaning.[9] But to be certain, one should consult reference works[10] to make sure if that is *genuinely* the case, since it may not be.

8.2 Present Middle Indicative

8.2.1 The Present Middle Indicative is an action that occurs in the speaker's present time ("present indicative") where the subject both does the action and receives the action ("middle"). Example: "I am on my guard."

8.2.2 *Table of Verb Tenses*

Tense	Aug/ Red	Tense stem	TF + CV	Endings	First singular
Pres act		pres	o/ε	prim act	λύω
Pres mid/pas		pres	o/ε	prim mid/pas	λύομαι

8.2.3 **Verbal Form of Present Middle Indicative**

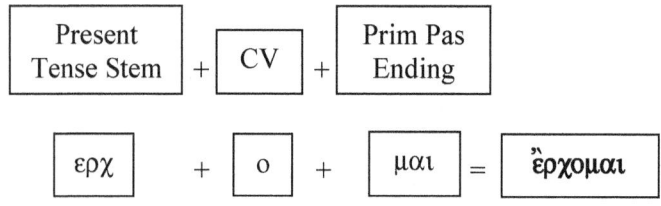

---

[7] Wallace, *GGBB*, 428.
[8] Ibid.
[9] For that reason, students should put "Dep" in the "Voice" column in their parsing charts in the workbook.
[10] E.g., Wallace, *GGBB*.

Chapter Eight: Present Middle/Passive Indicative and Contract Verbs

8.2.4 *Table of Verb Endings*

		Primary Endings		Secondary Endings	
Active Voice	Singular	λύω		ἔλυον	ν/α
		λύεις	ς	ἔλυες	ς
		λύει	ι	ἔλυε(ν)	(ν)
	Plural	λύομεν	μεν	ἐλύομεν	μεν
		λύετε	τε	ἐλύετε	τε
		λύουσι(ν)	σι	ἔλυον	ν
Midd/Pass Voice	Singular	λύομαι	μαι	ἐλυόμην	μην
		λύῃ	σαι	ἐλύου	σο
		λύεται	ται	ἐλύετο	το
	Plural	λυόμεθα	μεθα	ἐλυόμεθα	μεθα
		λύεσθε	σθε	ἐλύεσθε	σθε
		λύονται	νται	ἐλύοντο	ντο

8.2.5 **Paradigm of Present Middle Indicative**

	Form	Gloss	CV	Ending
1ˢᵗ Sg	ἔρχομαι	I am coming	ο	μαι
2ⁿᵈ Sg	ἔρχῃ	You are coming	ε	σαι
3ʳᵈ Sg	ἔρχεται	He, she, is coming	ε	ται
1ˢᵗ Pl	ἐρχόμεθα	We are coming	ο	μεθα
2ⁿᵈ Pl	ἔρχεσθε	You are coming	ε	σθε
3ʳᵈ Pl	ἔρχονται	They are coming	ο	νται

Example:

λέγω τούτῳ, Πορεύθητι, καὶ <u>πορεύεται</u>, καὶ ἄλλῳ, Ἔρχου, καὶ <u>ἔρχεται</u>.
I say to this one *Go!* and <u>he goes</u>, and to another *Come!* and <u>he comes</u>.[11]

---

[11] Mt 8:9.

8.3 Present Passive Indicative

8.3.1 The Present Passive Indicative is a completed action whose affects are felt in the speaker's present ("present indicative") where the subject receives the action ("passive"). Example: "I am being guarded."

8.3.2 Verbal Form of Present Passive Indicative

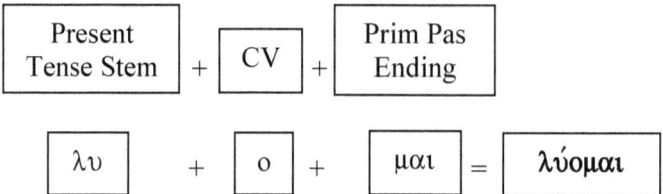

8.3.3 Paradigm of Present Passive Indicative

	Form	Gloss	CV	Ending
1ˢᵗ Sg	λύομαι	I am being released	ο	μαι
2ⁿᵈ Sg	λύῃ	You are being released	ε	σαι
3ʳᵈ Sg	λύεται	He, she, it is being released	ε	ται
1ˢᵗ Pl	λυόμεθα	We are being released	ο	μεθα
2ⁿᵈ Pl	λύεσθε	You are being released	ε	σθε
3ʳᵈ Pl	λύονται	They are being released	ο	νται

Examples:

Καὶ <u>συνάγονται</u> οἱ ἀπόστολοι πρὸς τὸν Ἰησοῦν, καὶ ἀπήγγειλαν αὐτῷ πάντα ὅσα ἐποίησαν καὶ ὅσα ἐδίδαξαν.
The apostles <u>were being gathered together</u> with Jesus; and they reported to Him all that they had done and taught.[12]

…καὶ <u>ἐβαπτίζοντο</u> ἐν τῷ Ἰορδάνῃ ποταμῷ ὑπ' αὐτοῦ ἐξομολογούμενοι τὰς ἁμαρτίας αὐτῶν
…and they <u>were [being] baptized</u> by him in the river Jordan, confessing their sins.[13]

---

[12] Mk 6:30. This can be rendered, "gathered together," but is not as accurate.

Chapter Eight: Present Middle/Passive Indicative and Contract Verbs

8.4 Contractions and Contract Verbs

8.4.1 Contractions are when letters or words combine into one unit. For example, "can not" in English can contract into "can't." Or, "will not," which contracts into "won't." English has lots of contractions especially in slang. For example, "runnin'" is the same as "running," and "I am going to" is the same as "I'm gonna." The verbs in all of these cases (can, will, run, go) might be referred to as "contract verbs," because those verbs contract.

8.4.2 In Greek, contract verbs are verbs that end in α, ε, or ο. When these final stem vowels come into contact with a connecting vowel, tense formative, or personal ending, the two vowels may contract. Example: ποιε + ομεν = ποιοῦμεν.

8.4.3 As seen in the above example, a circumflex accent (over the second vowel) indicates when a contraction has taken place.

8.4.4 Greek verbs only contract in the present and imperfect tenses.

8.4.5 There are **Ten Rules of Contraction**. The first five are common and must be memorized, while the last five are rare and do not have to be memorized.

---

[13] Mt 3:6.

8.4.6 The **Ten Rules of Contraction** are:
1. *ου is formed from εο, οε, and οο.*
   i. ποιέω + ο + μεν = ποιοῦμεν
   ii. πληρόω + ε + τε = πληροῦτε
2. *ει is formed from εε.*
   i. ποιέω + ε + τε = ποιεῖτε
3. *ω is formed from almost any combination of ο or ω with any other vowel.*
   i. ἀγαπάω + ο + μεν = αγαπῶμεν
4. *α is formed from αε.*
   i. ἀγαπάω + ε + τε = αγαπᾶτε
5. *ῃ is formed from εα, and from εε in compound verbs.*
   i. ποιέω + σαι = ποιῇ[14]
   ii. ε + ἐπερωτάω = ἐπηρώτάω
6. *οι is formed from οει.*
7. *Two identical vowels form a single vowel.* αα = α. The two exceptions are εε = ει and οο = ου.
8. *An ο or ω will replace an α, ε, or η regardless of their order.* αο and οα both = ω. The two exceptions are εο and οε, which both = ου.
9. *If a contract vowel and the first vowel of a dipthong are the same, they simplify.* οου = ου.
10. *If a contract vowel and the first vowel of a dipthong are different, the first vowel of dipthong contract according to the five rules.* εου = ου.

8.4.7 It is important to remember that the other rules for contraction (see the *Table of Stops and Fricatives* in chapter 3) still apply with verbs.

---

[14] The sigma drops out since it stands between two vowels.

Chapter Eight: Present Middle/Passive Indicative and Contract Verbs

Vocabulary

αἴρω	1) raise up, lift; 2) take away, remove, carry off, expel
ἀποκρίνομαι	answer, reply, counter, rejoin
ἀποκτείνω	kill
ἀποστέλλω	send, send away/out/off
βαπτίζω	a) wash, purify; b) immerse, dip, plunge, wash, baptize
βασιλεύς, -έως, ὁ	king, (chief) ruler
γεννάω	a) to father, beget, procreate; b) bear
δεῖ	one must, one needs, as need requires, one ought
δύναμαι	be able
ἔρχομαι	1) come, arrive; 2) go
ζάω and ζῶ	1-3) live
Ἰουδαῖος, -α, -ον	1) adj. Judean/Jewish; 2) n. Judean, Jew
Ἰουδαία, -ας, ἡ	Judea
Ἰσραήλ, ὁ	Israel
καρπός, -οῦ, ὁ	1) fruit; 2) fruit, produce, yield/gain
νύξ, νυκτός, ἡ	night
ὅλος, -η, -ον	all (of), whole, entire
ὅστις, ἥτις, ὅτι	rel. pron. 1) anyone who, whoever, whatever; 2) who, which, namely one (those) who
πορεύομαι or πορεύω[15]	1) go, make one's way, die; 2) conduct oneself, live, walk
προσκυνέω	do obeisance, pay homage, worship
συνάγω	1) gather; 2) take in as guest; 3) join in
τόπος, -ου, ὁ	1) place, space; 2) responsibility; 3) opportunity
ὡς	adv. 1) (just) as, (just) like, similar to, in the manner that/of, as (though) it were, as if, as; 2) as though, with the thought that, like; 3) how; 4) when, after, while, when, as long as, since, in order that, so that, about, nearly, close to

---

[15] *CL*, 293, has this representation, saying "in NT only as mid. and pass."

9 Imperfect Indicative and εἰμί

9.1 Imperfect Active Indicative

9.1.1 The Imperfect Active Indicative indicates a continuous action in the past. Example: "I was guarding."[1] Due to its specificity and less common use, interpreters of the New Testament should pay extra attention when they come across an imperfect verb.

9.1.2 The imperfect tense uses the secondary endings (see below). This means the imperfect tense also uses a prefix known as an "augment," which is an epsilon (ε) that comes before the verb stem.

9.1.3 In compound verbs where a preposition combines with a verb stem to form a single word, the augment comes after the preposition and before the verb stem.[2] This can cause contractions if the stem begins with a vowel.[3] Examples:

9.1.3.1 ἀπέρχομαι is a compound verb (απο + ἐρχομαι) meaning "I am departing." The imperfect would be ἀπήρχομαι (I was departing).

9.1.3.2 προσεύχομαι is a compound verb (προς + εὔχομαι) meaning "I am praying." The imperfect would be προσηύχετο ("he/she/it was departing.")

9.1.4 As the examples above show, the augment contracts into an η according to the fifth rule (ε + ε = η).

---

[1] Do not confuse the Imperfect with the Aorist Tense, which is simple past tense ("I guarded").

[2] When the preposition ends in a vowel, that vowel will usuall drop out before the agument. Example: κατέβαινομεν.

[3] If the stem of the verb begins with a consonant, the contractions caused by the augment can be irregular. For example, ἐξέβαλλον in Mark 6:13.

Chapter Nine: Imperfect Indicative and εἰμί

9.1.5 *Table of Verb Tenses*

Tense	Aug/ Red	Tense stem	TF + CV	Endings	First singular
Pres act		pres	o/ε	prim act	λύω
Pres mid/pas		pres	o/ε	prim mid/pas	λύομαι
Imperf act	ε	pres	o/ε	sec act	ἔλυον
Imperf mid/pas	ε	pres	o/ε	sec mid/pas	ἐλυόμην

9.1.6 **Verbal Form of Imperfect Active Indicative**

| Aug | + | Present Tense Stem | + | CV | + | Sec Act Ending |

| ἐ | + | λυ | + | ο | + | ν | = | ἔλυον |

9.1.7 *Table of Verb Endings*

		Primary Endings		*Secondary Endings*	
Active Voice Singular		λύω		ἔλυον	ν/α
		λύεις	ς	ἔλυες	ς
		λύει	ι	ἔλυε(ν)	(ν)
Active Voice Plural		λύομεν	μεν	ἐλύομεν	μεν
		λύετε	τε	ἐλύετε	τε
		λύουσι(ν)	σι	ἔλυον	ν
Midd/Pass Voice Singular		λύομαι	μαι	ἐλυόμην	μην
		λύῃ	σαι	ἐλύου	σο
		λύεται	ται	ἐλύετο	το
Midd/Pass Voice Plural		λυόμεθα	μεθα	ἐλυόμεθα	μεθα
		λύεσθε	σθε	ἐλύεσθε	σθε
		λύονται	νται	ἐλύοντο	ντο

9.1.8 Paradigm of Imperfect Active Indicative

	Form	Gloss	CV	Ending
1ˢᵗ Sg	ἔλυον	I was releasing	ο	ν
2ⁿᵈ Sg	ἔλυες	You were releasing	ε	ς
3ʳᵈ Sg	ἔλυε(ν)	He, she, it was releasing	ε	(ν)
1ˢᵗ Pl	ἐλύομεν	We were releasing	ο	μεν
2ⁿᵈ Pl	ἐλύετε	You (all) were releasing	ε	τε
3ʳᵈ Pl	ἔλυον	They were releasing	ο	σι

Examples:

Μετὰ ταῦτα ἦλθεν ὁ Ἰησοῦς καὶ οἱ μαθηταὶ αὐτοῦ εἰς τὴν Ἰουδαίαν γῆν, καὶ ἐκεῖ διέτριβεν μετ' αὐτῶν καὶ ἐβάπτιζεν.
After this Jesus and his disciples went into the Judean countryside, and he remained there with them and was baptizing.[4]

καὶ πᾶς ὁ ὄχλος ἤρχετο πρὸς αὐτόν, καὶ ἐδίδασκεν αὐτούς.
And all the people were coming to Him, and He was teaching them.[5]

9.2 Imperfect Middle/Passive Indicative

9.2.1 *Table of Verb Tenses*

Tense	Aug/Red	Tense stem	TF + CV	Endings	First singular
Present act		pres	o/ε	prim act	λύω
Present mid/pas		pres	o/ε	prim mid/pas	λύομαι
Imperfect act	ε	pres	o/ε	sec act	ἔλυον
Imperfect mid/pas	ε	pres	o/ε	sec mid/pas	ἐλυόμην

---

[4] Jn 3:22.
[5] Mk 2:13.

9.2.2 Verbal Form of Imperfect Middle/Passive Indicative

Aug + Present Tense Stem + CV + Sec Pas Ending

ἐ + λυ + ο + μην = ἐλυόμην

9.2.3 *Table of Verb Endings*

		Primary Endings		Secondary Endings	
Active Voice	Singular	λύω		ἔλυον	ν/α
		λύεις	ς	ἔλυες	ς
		λύει	ι	ἔλυε(ν)	(ν)
	Plural	λύομεν	μεν	ἐλύομεν	μεν
		λύετε	τε	ἐλύετε	τε
		λύουσι(ν)	σι	ἔλυον	ν
Midd/Pass Voice	Singular	λύομαι	μαι	ἐλυόμην	μην
		λύῃ	σαι	ἐλύου	σο
		λύεται	ται	ἐλύετο	το
	Plural	λυόμεθα	μεθα	ἐλυόμεθα	μεθα
		λύεσθε	σθε	ἐλύεσθε	σθε
		λύονται	νται	ἐλύοντο	ντο

9.2.4 Paradigm of Imperfect Middle/Passive Indicative

	Form	Gloss	CV	Ending
1ˢᵗ Sg	ἐλυόμην	I was being released	ο	μην
2ⁿᵈ Sg	ἐλύου	You were being released	ε	σο
3ʳᵈ Sg	ἐλύετο	He, she, it was being released	ε	το
1ˢᵗ Pl	ἐλυόμεθα	We were being released	ο	μεθα
2ⁿᵈ Pl	ἐλύεσθε	You (all) were being released	ε	σθε
3ʳᵈ Pl	ἐλύοντο	They were being released	ο	ντο

Examples:

καὶ ἐβαπτίζοντο ὑπ' αὐτοῦ ἐν τῷ Ἰορδάνῃ.

and <u>were being baptized</u> by him in the river Jordan.[6]

9.3 εἰμί

9.3.1 Εἰμί is the extremely common Greek verb meaning "to be." You have already learned several of the present and imperfect forms. Now it's time to learn all of them.

9.3.2 Present Tense Paradigm

	Form	Translation
1 sg	εἰμί	I am
2 sg	εἶ	You are
3 sg	ἐστί(ν)	He/she/it is
1 pl	ἐσμέν	We are
2 pl	ἐστέ	You (all) are
3 pl	εἰσί(ν)	They are

---

[6] Mk 1:5.

9.4 Table of εἰμί Verbs

	Imperfect	Present	Future	Subjunctive
1 sg	ἤμην	εἰμί		
2 sg	ἦς, ἦσθα	εἶ		
3 sg	ἦν	ἐστί(ν)		
1 pl	ἦμεν, ἤμεθα	ἐσμέν		
2 pl	ἦτε	ἐστέ		
3 pl	ἦσαν	εἰσί(ν)		

Vocabulary

ἄρτος, -ου, ὁ	1) bread, loaf (of bread); 2) bread, food
ἀκολουθέω	1) follow; 2) accompany
ἀποθνῄσκω	die
βάλλω	1) throw, sow, scatter, pour, spew/spit, drop; 2) put, apply, lay, swing, deposit; 3) break loose, rush
γῆ, γῆς, ἡ	1) earth; 2) people, humanity; 3) land, country, region, ground
γλῶσσα, -ης, ἡ	1) tongue; 2) tongue, language; 3) tongue
γίνομαι	1) be born, be produced; 2) be made, be performed, be done; 3) come to be, become, take place, happen, occur, arise, be, belong (to), now, turn out to be, prove to be, be, be there, appear, come, arrive
γινώσκω	1) know, learn of, find out; 2) think, understand, comprehend, perceive, notice, realize, conclude; 3) make acquaintance, recognize; 4) have intercourse
διδάσκω	teach, instruct
ἐγείρω	rise, raise; a) get up; b) awaken, rouse, raise, rise; c) rise, appear, go
εἰσέρχομαι	go/enter in/into
ἐκβάλλω	put out, drive out, reject, cast out, take out, release, send out, bring out, pass, turn *x* into, dispatch

ἐκεῖ	1) there; 2) thither, in that place
ἐξέρχομαι	go/come out/away
ἐπερωτάω	1) ask; 2) ask for, demand
ἐρωτάω	1) ask; 2) ask, request
εὑρίσκω	1) find, locate, come across, discover, turn out to be, obtain; 2) find
ἔτι	adv. 1) still, yet, anymore, anylonger, already/right; 2) yet, still
θέλω	1) wish to have, desire, want; 2) wish, have in mind, want, be ready, maintain; 3) like
κρίνω	1) prefer, favor; 2) judge, pass judgment on, condemn, go to court (with), press charges; 3) judge, come to a decision, decide, consider
λαμβάνω	1) act. take; 2) pass. receive, take, get, take (up)
λαός, -οῦ, ὁ	people
μένω	1) remain, stay; 2) await, wait for
ὁράω	1) see, appear, visit, look; 2) see, perceive, see to it that, take care of, see to (it), tend to (it)
οὔτε	neither…nor
περιπατέω	1) go about, walk about/around, walk; 2) walk, live
προσέρχομαι	a) go forward, come in, answer; b) go before; c) go ahead
προσεύχομαι	pray
πῦρ, -ός, τό	fire
σοφία, -ας, ἡ	wisdom
στόμα, -ατος, τό	mouth
συναγωγή, -ῆς, ἡ	1) synagogue; 2) assembly, synagogue; 3) meeting
σῴζω	save, rescue
Φαρισαῖος, -ου, ὁ	Pharisee
χρόνος, -ου, ὁ	1-2) time

10 Future Active/Middle and Stem/Root Changes

10.1 The Future Tense

10.1.1 The future tense indicates an action occurring in the future.

10.1.2 Scholars are divided about whether the future says anything about aspect, and which aspect is primary if it does.

10.1.2.1 Mounce says the future tense "is the one Greek tense in which aspect is secondary to time."[1]

10.1.2.2 Porter says the future tense is an "enigma" that "does not clearly convey verbal aspect…It is best described as conveying a sense of *expectation*."[2]

10.1.2.3 Similarly, Decker says, "The future-tense form expresses expectation, which is most commonly rendered in English as future time. The Greek future tense-form is actually more closely related to the category of mood than of tense.…The Greek future tense-form is probably best viewed as aspectually vague. That is, from the form alone it is not possible to say that the writer is viewing the situation either as a process, as a complete event, or as a state."[3]

10.1.2.4 Wallace, however, says "With reference to *aspect,* the future seems to offer an *external* portrayal, something of a temporal counterpart to the aorist indicative," and "Our view that the future is both a true aspect and an exclusively external one is based both on morphology and usage: Its formal link to the

---

[1] Mounce, *BBG*, 160.
[2] Porter, *Fundamentals*, 86.
[3] Decker, *Reading Koine Greek*, 309-10.

aorist suggests that it shares its aspect with the aorist (analogous to the imperfect sharing its aspect with the present, and the pluperfect with the perfect). This would make it a summary tense."[4]

10.1.3 Although one can never be certain, Wallace's observation suggests that, for all practical purposes, it may be best to translate the future with a simple aspect.[5] Example: "I will study" (instead of "I will be studying.")

10.2 Forms of the Future

10.2.1 Future verbs tend to be the *biggest* Greek words since they include both a tense formative *and* a connecting vowel.

$$\boxed{\text{Future Tense Stem}} + \boxed{\text{TF}} + \boxed{\text{CV}} + \boxed{\text{Ending}}$$

10.2.2 As you can see in the table below, the future tense can take on six different forms within the three major tenses. This is generally because there are two variations of the tense formative for each voice, one set for regular future verbs (σ and θησ), and the other for "liquid verbs" (εσ and ησ), which are stems that end in a "liquid" (λ, μ, ν, and ρ). We'll discuss this more below.

10.2.3 It is important to review the *Table of Stops and Fricatives* since the tense formative (σ) in the future can cause contractions.

	Stops	Fricatives		
		Hard	*Soft*	
Labial	π	φ	β	ψ
Velar	κ	χ	γ	ξ
Dental	τ	θ	δ	σ

---

[4] Wallace, *GGBB*, 566-67.
[5] My colleague Dr. Bret Saunders, a scholar in humanities and literature, finds the lack of complexity in the Greek future tense and the abundance of complexity in the past tense(s) unsurprising given the Greeks' preoccupation with the past.

Chapter Ten: Future Active/Middle and Stem/Root Changes

Examples:
a. βλεπ + σω = βλέψω (I will see)
b. αγ + σω = ἄξω (I will lead, bring, arrest)
c. βαπτιδ + σω = βαπτίσω (I will baptize)

10.3 Future Active Indicative
10.3.1 *Table of Verb Tenses*

Tense	Aug/ Red	Tense stem	TF + CV	Endings	First singular
Present act		pres	o/ε	prim act	λύω
Present mid/pas		pres	o/ε	prim mid/pas	λύομαι
Imperfect act	ε	pres	o/ε	sec act	ἔλυον
Imperfect mid/pas	ε	pres	o/ε	sec mid/pas	ἐλυόμην
Future act		fut act	σ/εσ + o/ε	prim act	λύσω μενῶ
Future mid		fut act	σ/εσ + o/ε	prim mid/pas	πορευσομαι μενουμαι
Future pas		aor pas	θη + o/ε	prim mid/pas	λυθησομαι ἀποσταλησομαι

10.3.2 Verbal Form of Future Active Indicative (Non-Liquid)

Future Active Tense Stem	+	TF (σ)	+	CV	+	Prim Act Ending

| λυ | + | σ | + | ο | + | μεν | = | λύσομεν |

10.3.3 Paradigm of Future Active Indicative (Non-Liquid)

	Form	Gloss	TF	CV	Ending
1st Sg	λύσω	I will release	σ	ο	
2nd Sg	λύσεις	You will release	σ	ε	ς
3rd Sg	λύσει	He, she, it will release	σ	ε	ι
1st Pl	λύσομεν	We will release	σ	ο	μεν
2nd Pl	λύσετε	You (all) will release	σ	ε	τε
3rd Pl	λύσουσι(ν)	They will release	σ	ο	σι

Examples:

τέξεται δὲ υἱόν, καὶ <u>καλέσεις</u> τὸ ὄνομα αὐτοῦ Ἰησοῦν· αὐτὸς γὰρ <u>σώσει</u> τὸν λαὸν αὐτοῦ ἀπὸ τῶν ἁμαρτιῶν αὐτῶν.
 She will bear a son, and <u>you are to name</u> him Jesus, for <u>he will save</u> his people from their sins.[6]

μετὰ τὰς ἡμέρας ἐκείνας, λέγει κύριος· διδοὺς νόμους μου ἐπὶ καρδίας αὐτῶν καὶ ἐπὶ τὴν διάνοιαν αὐτῶν <u>ἐπιγράψω</u> αὐτούς,
This is the covenant that I will make with them after those days, says the Lord: I will put my laws in their hearts and <u>I will write</u> them on their minds.[7]

---

[6] Mt 1:21.
[7] Hb 10:16.

Chapter Ten: Future Active/Middle and Stem/Root Changes

10.3.4 *Liquid* **Future Active Indicative**

10.3.4.1 "Liquid" verbs function the same way as non-liquid verbs. They just have a different form.

10.3.4.2 As mentioned above, Greek "liquids" are the consonants λ, μ, ν, and ρ. Liquid verbs have a stem ending with one of these liquids.

10.3.4.3 Given the σ in the tense formative of the liquids, it is important to note that the sigma usually drops out when it stands between two vowels (see 10.2.5 below for an example), typically causing a contraction.

10.3.5 Verbal Form of *Liquid* Future Active Indicative

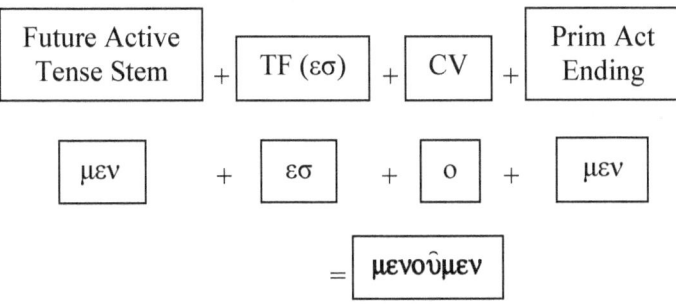

10.3.6 Paradigm of *Liquid* Future Active Indicative

	Form	Gloss	TF	CV	Ending
1st Sg	μενῶ	I will remain	εσ	ο	
2nd Sg	μενεῖς	You will remain	εσ	ε	ς
3rd Sg	μενεῖ	He, she, it will remain	εσ	ε	ι
1st Pl	μενοῦμεν	We will remain	εσ	ο	μεν
2nd Pl	μενεῖτε	You (all) will remain	εσ	ε	τε
3rd Pl	μενοῦσι(ν)	They will remain	εσ	ο	σι

Examples:

καὶ τοῦτο πεποιθὼς οἶδα ὅτι μενῶ καὶ παραμενῶ πᾶσιν ὑμῖν εἰς τὴν ὑμῶν προκοπὴν καὶ χαρὰν τῆς πίστεως.
Convinced of this, I know that I will remain and continue with you all for your progress and joy in the faith.[8]

ἐν τῷ ὀνόματί μου δαιμόνια ἐκβαλοῦσιν,
…in My name they will cast out demons;[9]

τέξεται δὲ υἱόν, καὶ καλέσεις τὸ ὄνομα αὐτοῦ Ἰησοῦν· αὐτὸς γὰρ σώσει τὸν λαὸν αὐτοῦ ἀπὸ τῶν ἁμαρτιῶν αὐτῶν.
 She will bear a son, and you are to name him Jesus, for he will save his people from their sins.[10]

10.4 Future Middle Indicative

10.4.1 Remember from previous chapters that only present tense and imperfect tense verbs in the middle voice are deponent. This means all other tenses in the middle voice (including the future) express an action where the subject both performs and receives the action. Since the middle is distinguished from the passive in this way, it is necessary to look at each form of the middle voice in each tense. In this section, we will look at the future middle verb.

---

[8] Phil 1:25.
[9] Mk 16:17.
[10] Mt 1:21.

10.4.2 *Table of Verb Tenses*

Tense	Aug/ Red	Tense stem	TF + CV	Endings	First singular
Present act		pres	ο/ε	prim act	λύω
Present mid/pas		pres	ο/ε	prim mid/pas	λύομαι
Imperfect act	ε	pres	ο/ε	sec act	ἔλυον
Imperfect mid/pas	ε	pres	ο/ε	sec mid/pas	ἐλυόμην
Future act		fut act	σ/εσ + ο/ε	prim act	λύσω μενῶ
Future mid		fut act	σ/εσ + ο/ε	prim mid/pas	πορεύσομαι μενοῦμαι
Future pas		aor pas	θη + ο/ε	prim mid/pas	λυθήσομαι ἀποσταλήσομαι

10.4.3 Verbal Form of Future Middle Indicative (Non-Liquid)

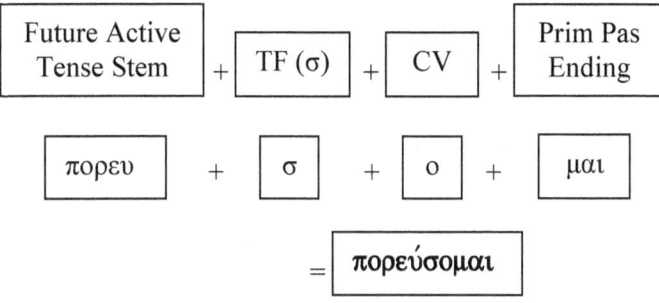

10.4.4 Paradigm of Future Middle Indicative

	Form	Gloss	TF	CV	Ending
1st Sg	πορεύσομαι	I will go	σ	ο	μαι
2nd Sg	πορεύσῃ	You will go	σ	ε	σαι
3rd Sg	πορεύσεται	He, she, it will go	σ	ε	ται
1st Pl	πορευσόμεθα	We will go	σ	ο	μεθα
2nd Pl	πορεύσεσθε	You (all) will go	σ	ε	σθε
3rd Pl	πορεύσονται	They will go	σ	ο	νται

Examples:

καὶ <u>ἀπελεύσονται</u> οὗτοι εἰς κόλασιν αἰώνιον...
And these <u>will go away</u> into eternal punishment...[11]

κἀκεῖ με <u>ὄψονται</u>.
there <u>they will see</u> me.[12]

Τίς ἐξ ὑμῶν ἕξει φίλον καὶ <u>πορεύσεται</u>[13] πρὸς αὐτὸν μεσονυκτίου καὶ εἴπῃ αὐτῷ, Φίλε, χρῆσόν μοι τρεῖς ἄρτους.
Which of you who has a friend <u>will go</u> to him at midnight and say to him, "Friend, lend me three loaves."[14]

Καὶ εἶπεν Ζαχαρίας πρὸς τὸν ἄγγελον, Κατὰ τί <u>γνώσομαι</u> τοῦτο;
Zechariah said to the angel, "How <u>will I know</u> that this is so?[15]

10.4.5 Verbal Form of *Liquid* Future Middle Indicative

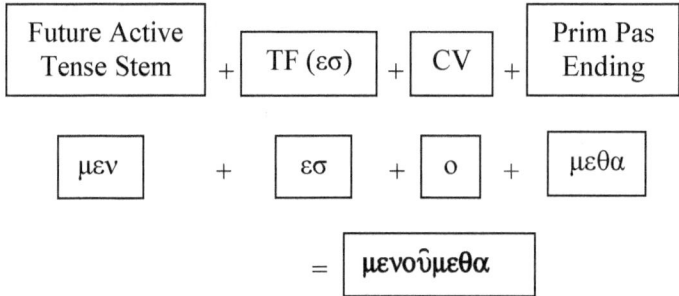

---

[11] Mt 25:46a.
[12] Mt 28:10b.
[13] Recall that deponent verbs only apply for the present tense stem (8.1.4).
[14] Lk 11:5 (ESV).
[15] Lk 1:18a.

10.4.6 Paradigm of *Liquid* Future Middle Indicative

	Form	Gloss	TF	CV	Ending
1st Sg	μενοῦμαι	I will remain	εσ	ο	μαι
2nd Sg	μενῇ	You will remain	εσ	ε	σαι
3rd Sg	μενεῖται	He, she, it will remain	εσ	ε	ται
1st Pl	μενούμεθα	We will remain	εσ	ο	μεθα
2nd Pl	μενεῖσθε	You (all) will remain	εσ	ε	σθε
3rd Pl	μενοῦνται	They will remain	εσ	ο	νται

Examples:

...καὶ ζητήσετέ με, καὶ ἐν τῇ ἁμαρτίᾳ ὑμῶν <u>ἀποθανεῖσθε</u>.
...and you will seek Me, and <u>you will die</u> in your sin.[16]

10.5 Stem Changes

10.5.1 Before moving on to the final future tenses (Future Passive), it is necessary to cover some of the last major rules for Greek verbs.

10.5.2 Even though the present tense stem is the lexical form that you memorize, the present tense stem is actually the most irregular.[17] When a verb goes from present to future tense, for example, the stem often changes. In English "I run" changes to "I ran" when going from the present to the past time. The same is true for Greek. Example: the present tense "I raise" is αἴρω while the future tense "I will raise" is ἀρῶ. (The present tense has an additional iota.) This does not mean, of course, that *every* time a Greek verb appears in a different tense it has different stem.

10.5.3 There are six tense stems (which correspond with the *Table of Verb Tenses*).[18]

---

[16] Jn 8:21.
[17] This isn't to say that the present tense is rarely used. On the contrary, there are 11,563 present-tense verbs (and verbals), 11,585 aorists, 1680 imperfects, 1627 futures, 1572 perfects, and 86 pluperfects in the NT. Thus, Porter in *Fundamentals*, 36, says the aorist tense "is the most widely used tense-form in Greek."
[18] Some grammarians, like Porter, consolidate these six into "three major tense-forms"—present, perfect, and aorist.

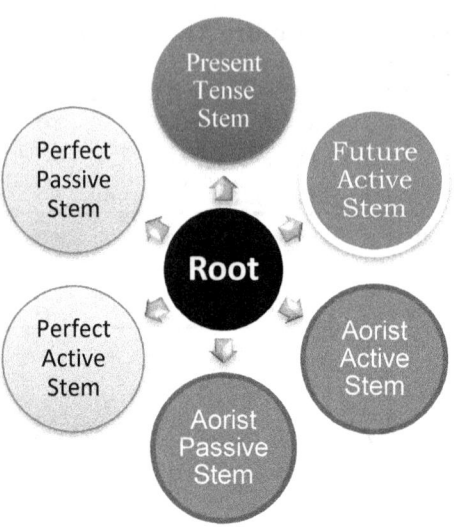

10.5.4 To help you learn how to read and understand Greek efficiently, we will learn the most common patterns of stem changes when moving from the lexical form (present tense) to other tense stems. This will help you identify words across all the whole range of Greek verbs. The examples below use the present and future active tense stems, but the changes are commonly found thourghout several of the Greek tenses.

10.5.4.1 Removing from a Double Consonant

ἀποστέλλῶ → ἀποστέλῶ

10.5.4.2 Removing an ι

ἐγείρῶ → ἐγερῶ

10.5.4.3 Removing an σκ

ἀποθνήσκω → ἀποθανοῦμαι

10.6 Root Changes

10.6.1 Sometimes the entire root of a verb changes when switching tenses. In English these are usually called "irregular verbs," like when "bring" becomes "brought," or "go" becomes "went." Example: the present tense root of λέγω is λεγ, but the future tense root of λέγω is ελευθ. Even though the root of the word is completely different, the meaning of the word doesn't change (except with respect to the tense, of course).

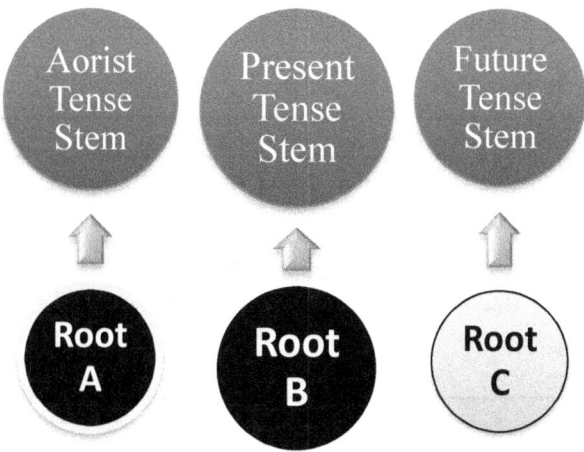

10.6.2 Fortunately, there are only nine cases in the New Testament where words have different roots in the future tense. You only need to memorize the five most common. They can be memorized in the *Table of Root Changes*.

10.6.3 *Table of Root Changes*

Aorist	Present (Lex)	Future
ἦλθον	ἔρχομαι	ἐλεύσομαι
εἶπον	λέγω	ἐρῶ
εἶδον	ὁράω	ὄψομαι
εφαγον	εσθίω	φάγομαι
ἤνεγκα	φερω	οἴσω

10.6.3.1 Examples:

ὁράω = I am seeing   ἔρχομαι = I am coming/going
ὄψομαι = I will see   ἦλθον = I went

Σὺ εἶπας· πλὴν λέγω ὑμῖν, ἀπ' ἄρτι <u>ὄψεσθε</u> τὸν υἱὸν τοῦ ἀνθρώπου καθήμενον ἐκ δεξιῶν τῆς δυνάμεως...
You have said so. But I tell you, From now on <u>you will see</u> the Son of Man seated at the right hand of Power...[19]

10.7 Table of *εἰμί* Verbs

	Imperfect	Present	Future	Subjunctive
1 sg	ἤμην	εἰμί	ἔσομαι	ὦ
2 sg	ἦς, ἦσθα	εἶ	ἔσῃ	ᾖς
3 sg	ἦν	ἐστί(ν)	ἔσται	ᾖ
1 pl	ἦμεν, ἤμεθα	ἐσμέν	ἐσόμεθα	ὦμεν
2 pl	ἦτε	ἐστέ	ἔσεσθε	ἦτε
3 pl	ἦσαν	εἰσί(ν)	ἔσονται	ὦσι(ν)

Example:

σὺ οὖν ἐὰν προσκυνήσῃς ἐνώπιον ἐμοῦ, <u>ἔσται</u> σοῦ πᾶσα.
Therefore if you worship before me, <u>it will be</u> all yours (Hübner).[20]

<u>ἔσονται</u> γὰρ ἀπὸ τοῦ νῦν πέντε ἐν ἑνὶ οἴκῳ διαμεμερισμένοι, τρεῖς ἐπὶ δυσὶν καὶ δύο ἐπὶ τρισίν...
From now on five in one household <u>will be</u> divided, three against two and two against three...[21]

---

[19] Mt 26:64a.
[20] Lk 4:7.
[21] Lk 12:52.

Chapter Ten: Future Active/Middle and Stem/Root Changes

Vocabulary

ἄγω	1) lead, bring, carry, take; 2) spend, hold; 3) to go
αἷμα, -ατος, τό	blood, human being
αἰτέω	ask, ask for, request
ἄρχω	1) act. rule; 2) begin
ἀπέρχομαι	go, go away/off, depart, leave
γράφω	write, inscribe
διό	conj. therefore, for this reason
δοξάζω	glorify
δύναμις, -εως, ἡ	1) power, might; 2) powerful/wondrous deed, miracle; 3) power[22]
ἕκαστος, -η, -ον	each, every; n. each one, every one
ἱμάτιον, -ου, τό	a) clothing, apparel; b) cloak, coat
κηρύσσω	proclaim
μᾶλλον	1) (much) more, all the more, still more; 2) rather, instead
μαρτυρέω	testify, attest
ὄρος, ὄρους, τό	hill, mount, mountain
πίνω	drink
ὑπάγω	a) go away, leave; b) go, be on one's way
φοβέομαι	1) be afraid, fear, be afraid of, be apprehensive/worried about; 2) have deep respect (for), be filled with awe
χαίρω	1) be happy/glad/delighted, rejoice; 2) greetings

---

[22] It would be wise to avoid the use of "miracle" since it is a philosophically loaded term in our modern and post-modern world, typically presuming a dualism of the "natural" and "supernatural" world (with miracles, God, and "spiritual" things being associated with the latter and isolated from the former). In Christian theology, the whole universe is considered God's "playground" as it were, and not just part of it. ("Nature is what God does," as Augustine put it, or, the universe is the "theatre of God's glory," as Calvin put it.) See William Placher, *The Domestication of Transcendence: How Modern Thinking About God Went Wrong* (Louisville: WJK, 1996).

11 Future Passive and Aorist

11.1 The Future Passive Tense

11.1.1 As you can tell from the *Table of Verb Tenses* below, the future passive is different from other future tenses in that it has an aorist stem. Because they share stems in this way, this chapter combines the future passive with the aorist.

11.1.2 The future passive tense is also different from the other forms of the future in that it retains two different tense formatives *but they do not necessarily correspond to liquid words*. For example, θήσ and ήσ may be used in a liquid or non-liquid verb. For that reason, grammarians speak of "first" and "second" future passive, instead of "regular" and "liquid" future passive.

11.2 Future Passive Indicative

11.2.1 *Table of Verb Tenses*

Tense	Aug/ Red	Tense stem	TF + CV	Endings	First singular
Present act		pres	o/ε	prim act	λύω
Present mid/pas		pres	o/ε	prim mid/pas	λύομαι
Imperfect act	ε	pres	o/ε	sec act	ἔλυον
Imperfect mid/pas	ε	pres	o/ε	sec mid/pas	ἐλυόμην
Future act		fut act	σ/εσ + o/ε	prim act	λύσω μενῶ
Future mid		fut act	σ/εσ + o/ε	prim mid/pas	πορεύσομαι μενοῦμαι
Future pas		aor pas	θη/η + o/ε	prim mid/pas	λυθήσομαι ἀποσταλήσομαι

11.2.2 Verbal Form of 1ˢᵗ Future Passive Indicative

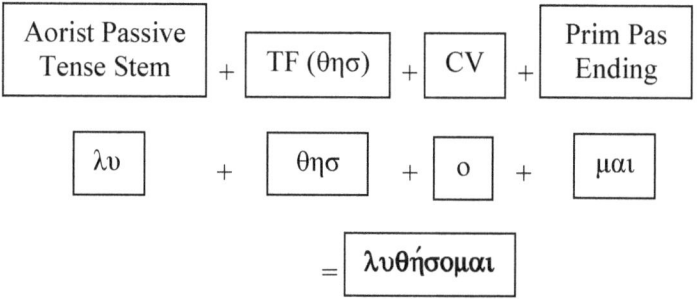

= λυθήσομαι

11.2.3 Paradigm of 1ˢᵗ Future Passive Indicative

	Form	Gloss	TF	CV	Ending
1ˢᵗ Sg	λυθήσομαι	I will be released	θησ	ο	μαι
2ⁿᵈ Sg	λυθήσῃ	You will be released	θησ	ε	σαι
3ʳᵈ Sg	λυθήσεται	He, she, it will be released	θησ	ε	ται
1ˢᵗ Pl	λυθησόμεθα	We will be released	θησ	ο	μεθα
2ⁿᵈ Pl	λυθήσεσθε	You (all) will be released	θησ	ε	σθε
3ʳᵈ Pl	λυθήσονται	They will be released	θησ	ο	νται

Examples:

ὁ δὲ ἀγαπῶν με <u>ἀγαπηθήσεται</u> ὑπὸ τοῦ πατρός μου, κἀγὼ ἀγαπήσω αὐτὸν καὶ ἐμφανίσω αὐτῷ ἐμαυτόν.
And the one loving me <u>will be loved</u> by my Father, and I will love him and will disclose Myself to him. (Hübner)[1]

βασίλισσα νότου <u>ἐγερθήσεται</u> ἐν τῇ κρίσει μετὰ τῆς γενεᾶς ταύτης καὶ κατακρινεῖ αὐτήν,
The queen of the South <u>will be risen up</u> at the judgment with this generation and condemn it, (Hübner)[2]

---

[1] Jn 14:21b.
[2] Mt 12:42.

11.2.4 Verbal Form of 2nd Future Passive Indicative

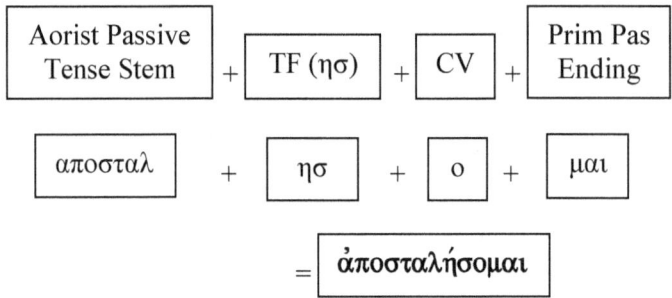

11.2.5 Paradigm of 2nd Future Passive Indicative

	Form	Gloss	TF	CV	Ending
1st Sg	ἀποσταλήσομαι	I will be sent	ησ	ο	μαι
2nd Sg	ἀποσταλήσῃ	You will be sent	ησ	ε	σαι
3rd Sg	ἀποσταλήσεται	He, she, it will be sent	ησ	ε	ται
1st Pl	ἀποσταλησόμεθα	We will be sent	ησ	ο	μεθα
2nd Pl	ἀποσταλήσεσθε	You (all) will be sent	ησ	ε	σθε
3rd Pl	ἀποσταλήσονται	They will be sent	ησ	ο	νται

Examples:

…γενήσεται αὐτοῖς παρὰ τοῦ πατρός μου τοῦ ἐν οὐρανοῖς.
…<u>it shall be done</u> for them by my Father who is in heaven.[3]

οἱ καταλείποντες κύριον ἐμπεσοῦνται εἰς αὐτήν, καὶ ἐν αὐτοῖς ἐκκαήσεται καὶ οὐ μὴ σβεσθῇ, <u>ἐπαποσταλήσεται</u> αὐτοῖς ὡς λέων καὶ ὡς πάρδαλις λυμανεῖται αὐτούς.
Those who forsake the Lord will fall into its power; it will burn among them and will not be put out. <u>It will be sent out</u> against them like a lion; like a leopard it will mangle them.[4]

---

[3] Mt 18:19.
[4] Sir 28:23 (LXX).

Chapter Eleven: Future Passive and Aorist

11.3 The Aorist Tense

11.3.1 The aorist tense indicates a simple action (aspect) occurring in the past (time). Example: "I slept" or "I ran." It is the most common verb tense in Koiné Greek.

11.3.2 The aorist tense is similar to the imperfect in that it has an augment and uses the secondary endings.

11.3.3 The aorist tense has more forms than any other Greek verb because it alternates between tense formatives and connecting vowels. Unlike the future, however, the aorist never combines *both* a tense formative *and* a connecting vowel.

11.4 Aorist Active Indicative

11.4.1 *Table of Verb Tenses*

Tense	Aug/ Red	Tense stem	TF + CV	Endings	First singular
Present act		pres	ο/ε	prim act	λύω
Present mid/pas		pres	ο/ε	prim mid/pas	λύομαι
Imperfect act	ε	pres	ο/ε	sec act	ἔλυον
Imperfect mid/pas	ε	pres	ο/ε	sec mid/pas	ἐλυόμην
Future act		fut act	σ/εσ + ο/ε	prim act	λύσω μενῶ
Future mid		fut act	σ/εσ + ο/ε	prim mid/pas	πορεύσομαι μενοῦμαι
Future pas		aor pas	θησ/ησ + ο/ε	prim mid/pas	λυθήσομαι ἀποσταλήσομαι
Aorist act	ε	aor act	σα/α / ο/ε	sec act	ἔλυσα ἔμεινα ἔλαβον
Aorist mid	ε	aor act	σα/α / ο/ε	sec mid/pas	ἐλυσάμην ἐγενόμην
Aorist pas	ε	aor pas	θη/η	sec act	ἐλύθην ἐγράφην

11.4.2 Verbal Form of 1ˢᵗ Aorist Active Indicative

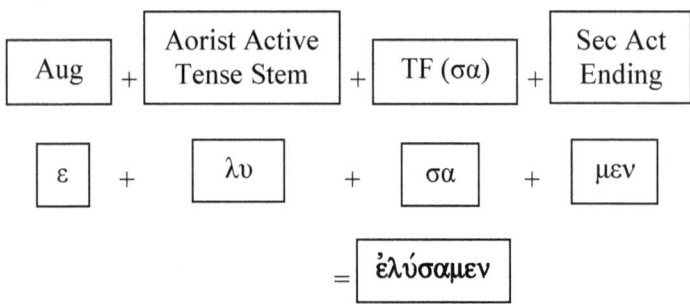

11.4.3 Paradigm of 1ˢᵗ Aorist Active Indicative

	Form	Gloss	TF	CV	Ending
1ˢᵗ Sg	ἔλυσα	I released	σα		ν/α
2ⁿᵈ Sg	ἔλυσας	You released	σα		ς
3ʳᵈ Sg	ἔλυσε(ν)	He, she, it released	σα		(ν)
1ˢᵗ Pl	ἐλύσαμεν	We released	σα		μεν
2ⁿᵈ Pl	ἐλύσατε	You (all) released	σα		τε
3ʳᵈ Pl	ἔλυσαν	They released	σα		ν

Examples:

πολλοὶ <u>ἐπίστευσαν</u> εἰς τὸ ὄνομα αὐτοῦ, θεωροῦντες αὐτοῦ τὰ σημεῖα ἃ ἐποίει·
…many <u>believed</u> in His name, observing His signs which He was doing.[5]

ὁ δὲ Ἰησοῦς <u>εἶπεν</u> αὐτοῖς, Πρὸς τὴν σκληροκαρδίαν ὑμῶν <u>ἔγραψεν</u> ὑμῖν τὴν ἐντολὴν ταύτην.
But Jesus <u>said</u> to them, "Because of your hardness of heart <u>he wrote</u> to you (all) this commandment." (Hübner)[6]

---

[5] Jn 2:23.
[6] Mk 10:5.

Chapter Eleven: Future Passive and Aorist

11.4.4 Verbal Form of *Liquid* Aorist Active Indicative

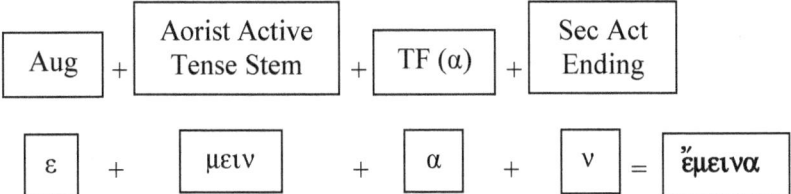

11.4.5 Paradigm of *Liquid* Aorist Active Indicative

	Form	Gloss	TF	CV	Ending
1st Sg	ἔμεινα	I remained	α		ν/α
2nd Sg	ἔμεινας	You remained	α		ς
3rd Sg	ἔμεινε(ν)	He, she, it remained	α		(ν)
1st Pl	ἐμείναμεν	We remained	α		μεν
2nd Pl	ἐμείνατε	You (all) remained	α		τε
3rd Pl	ἔμειναν	They remained	α		ν

Examples:

Ἔμεινεν δὲ Μαριὰμ σὺν αὐτῇ ὡς μῆνας τρεῖς, καὶ ὑπέστρεψεν εἰς τὸν οἶκον αὐτῆς.
And Mary stayed with her about three months, and then returned to her home.[7]

---

[7] Lk 1:56.

11.4.6 Verbal Form of 2nd Aorist Active Indicative

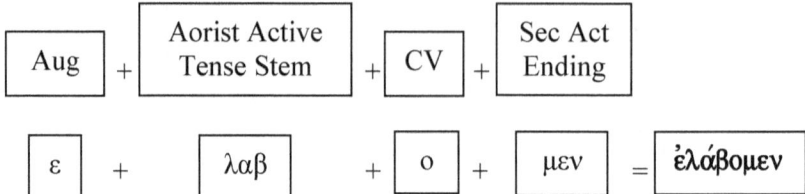

| Aug | + | Aorist Active Tense Stem | + | CV | + | Sec Act Ending |

ε + λαβ + ο + μεν = ἐλάβομεν

11.4.7 Paradigm of 2nd Aorist Active Indicative

	Form	Gloss	TF	CV	Ending
1ˢᵗ Sg	ἔλαβον	I took		ο	ν/α
2ⁿᵈ Sg	ἔλαβες	You took		ε	ς
3ʳᵈ Sg	ἔλαβε(ν)	He, she, it took		ε	(ν)
1ˢᵗ Pl	ἐλάβομεν	We took		ο	μεν
2ⁿᵈ Pl	ἐλάβετε	You (all) took		ε	τε
3ʳᵈ Pl	ἔλαβον	They took		ο	ν

Examples:

ἔλαβεν τοὺς ἑπτὰ ἄρτους καὶ τοὺς ἰχθύας καὶ εὐχαριστήσας ἔκλασεν καὶ ἐδίδου τοῖς μαθηταῖς, οἱ δὲ μαθηταὶ τοῖς ὄχλοις.

He took the seven loaves and the fish and giving thanks he broke them and started giving them to the disciples, and the disciples to the people. (Hübner)[8]

---

[8] Mt 15:36.

Chapter Eleven: Future Passive and Aorist

11.5 Aorist Middle Indicative
11.5.1 *Table of Verb Tenses*

Tense	Aug/ Red	Tense stem	TF + CV	Endings	First singular
Present act		pres	o/ε	prim act	λύω
Present mid/pas		pres	o/ε	prim mid/pas	λύομαι
Imperfect act	ε	pres	o/ε	sec act	ἔλυον
Imperfect mid/pas	ε	pres	o/ε	sec mid/pas	ἐλυόμην
Future act		fut act	σ/εσ + o/ε	prim act	λύσω μενῶ
Future mid		fut act	σ/εσ + o/ε	prim mid/pas	πορεύσομαι μενοῦμαι
Future pas		aor pas	θησ/ησ + o/ε	prim mid/pas	λυθήσομαι ἀποσταλήσομαι
Aorist act	ε	aor act	σα/α / o/ε	sec act	ἔλυσα ἔμεινα ἔλαβον
Aorist mid	ε	aor act	σα / o/ε	sec mid/pas	ἐλυσάμην ἐγενόμην
Aorist pas	ε	aor pas	θη/η	sec act	ἐλύθην ἐγράφην

11.5.2 Verbal Form of 1st Aorist Middle Indicative

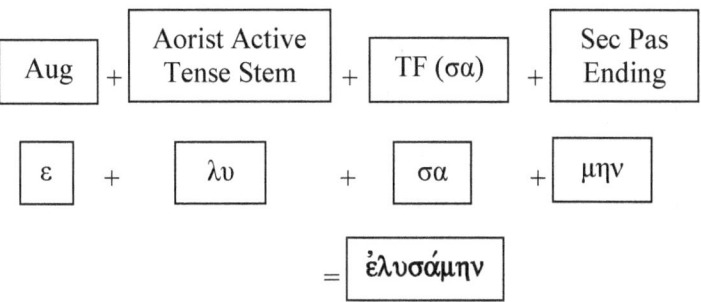

11.5.3 Paradigm of 1st Aorist Middle Indicative

	Form	Gloss	TF	CV	Ending
1st Sg	ἐλυσάμην	I released	σα		μην
2nd Sg	ἐλύσω	You released	σα		σο
3rd Sg	ἐλύσατο	He, she, it released	σα		το
1st Pl	ἐλυσάμεθα	We released	σα		μεθα
2nd Pl	ἐλύσασθε	You (all) released	σα		σθε
3rd Pl	ἐλύσαντο	They released	σα		ντο

Examples:

καὶ ἤρξαντο τίλλειν στάχυας καὶ ἐσθίειν.
…and they began to pluck heads of grain and to eat.[9]

11.5.4 Verbal Form of 2nd Aorist Middle Indicative

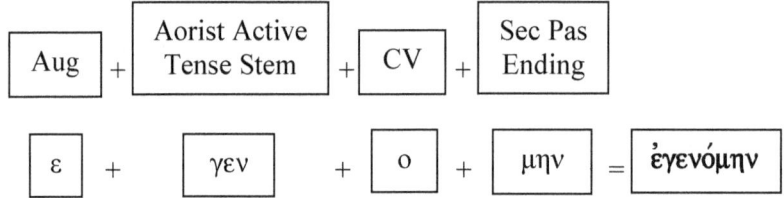

11.5.5 Paradigm of 2nd Aorist Middle Indicative

	Form	Gloss	TF	CV	Ending
1st Sg	ἐγενόμην	I became		ο	μην
2nd Sg	ἐγένου	You became		ε	σο
3rd Sg	ἐγένετο	He, she, it became		ε	το
1st Pl	ἐγενόμεθα	We became		ο	μεθα
2nd Pl	ἐγένεσθε	You (all) became		ε	σθε
3rd Pl	ἐγένοντο	They became		ο	ντο

---

[9] Mt 12:1, ESV.

Examples:

καὶ ἐγενόμην τοῖς Ἰουδαίοις ὡς Ἰουδαῖος, ἵνα Ἰουδαίους κερδήσω
To the Judeans I became as a Judean, so that I might win Judeans.[10]

11.6 Aorist Passive Indicative

11.6.1 The aorist passive has two irregularities that you should be aware of. First, instead of using the mid/passive endings (as one would expect), it paradoxically uses the active endings. Second, the 3rd plural ending can be σαν instead of simply ν.

11.6.2 *Table of Verb Tenses*

Tense	Aug/ Red	Tense stem	TF + CV	Endings	First singular
Present act		pres	o/ε	prim act	λύω
Present mid/pas		pres	o/ε	prim mid/pas	λύομαι
Imperfect act	ε	pres	o/ε	sec act	ἔλυον
Imperfect mid/pas	ε	pres	o/ε	sec mid/pas	ἐλυόμην
Future act		fut act	σ/εσ + o/ε	prim act	λύσω μενῶ
Future mid		fut act	σ/εσ + o/ε	prim mid/pas	πορεύσομαι μενοῦμαι
Future pas		aor pas	θησ/ησ + o/ε	prim mid/pas	λυθήσομαι ἀποσταλήσομαι
Aorist act	ε	aor act	σα/α / o/ε	sec act	ἔλυσα ἔμεινα ἔλαβον
Aorist mid	ε	aor act	σα / o/ε	sec mid/pas	ἐλυσάμην ἐγενόμην
Aorist pas	ε	aor pas	θη/η	sec act	ἐλύθην ἐγράφην

---

[10] 1 Cor 9:20.

11.6.3 Verbal Form of 1st Aorist Passive Indicative

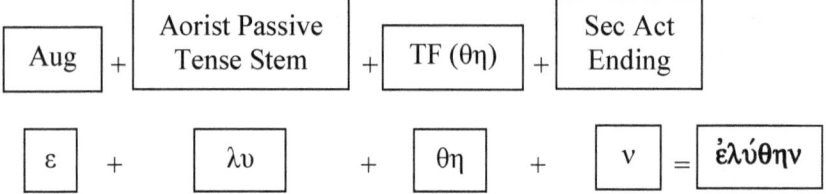

11.6.4 Paradigm of 1st Aorist Passive Indicative

	Form	Gloss	TF	CV	Ending
1st Sg	ἐλύθην	I was released	θη		ν/α
2nd Sg	ἐλύθης	You were released	θη		ς
3rd Sg	ἐλύθη	He, she, it was released	θη		(ν)
1st Pl	ἐλύθημεν	We were released	θη		μεν
2nd Pl	ἐλύθητε	You (all) were released	θη		τε
3rd Pl	ἐλύθησαν	They were released	θη		ν

Examples:

ἀπὸ δὲ τοῦ φόβου αὐτοῦ ἐσείσθησαν οἱ τηροῦντες καὶ <u>ἐγενήθησαν</u> ὡς νεκροί.

The guards shook for fear of him and <u>became</u> like dead men.[11]

---

[11] Mt 28:4.

11.6.5 Verbal Form of 2ⁿᵈ Aorist Passive Indicative

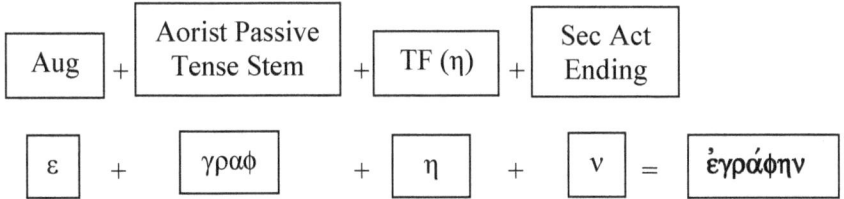

11.6.6 Paradigm of 2ⁿᵈ Aorist Passive Indicative

	Form	Gloss	TF	CV	Ending
1ˢᵗ Sg	ἐγράφην	I was written	η		ν/α
2ⁿᵈ Sg	ἐγράφης	You were written	η		ς
3ʳᵈ Sg	ἐγράφη	He, she, it was written	η		(ν)
1ˢᵗ Pl	ἐγράφημεν	We were written	η		μεν
2ⁿᵈ Pl	ἐγράφητε	You (all) were written	η		τε
3ʳᵈ Pl	ἐγράφησαν	They were written	η		σαν

Examples:

ἢ δι' ἡμᾶς πάντως λέγει; δι' ἡμᾶς γὰρ <u>ἐγράφη</u>, ὅτι ὀφείλει ἐπ' ἐλπίδι ὁ ἀροτριῶν ἀροτριᾶν, καὶ ὁ ἀλοῶν ἐπ' ἐλπίδι τοῦ μετέχειν.

Or is He speaking altogether for us? Yes, for our sake <u>it was written</u>, because the plowman ought to plow in hope and the thresher to thresh in hope of sharing the crops. (Hübner)[12]

---

[12] 1 Cor 9:10.

Vocabulary

ἀναβαίνω	go up
ἀρχιερεύς, -έως, ὁ	1) high priest, chief priest; 2) chief priests
ἀσπάζομαι	1) greet, say good-bye to, say farewell
γραμματεύς, -έως, ὁ	1) secretary (of state), clerk; 2) legal scholar, teacher of the law
δεξιός, -ιά, -ιόν	right
δέχομαι	receive
δοκέω	1) think, opine, regard/recognize, decide, resolve; 2) seem (good)
δύο	two
ἐσθίω	1) eat; 2) eat, devour, consume
ἕτερος, -α, -ον	1) other, another; 2) other, another, different
εὐαγγελίζω	1) bring/announce good news; 2) publish good news/tidings, publish the good news, publish the gospel
θεωρέω	1) look at, observe, watch, behold, Catch sight of, take notice of; 2) infer, see, perceive, experience
ἱερόν, -οῦ, τό	sanctuary, temple
κάθημαι	sit (down), take a seat
καταβαίνω	come/go down
κράζω	1) scream, cry out; 2) call out
οὐχι	not, no
παιδίον, -ου, τό	child
παρακαλέω	1) invite, entreat, implore; 2) comfort, console; 3) urge, exhort, encourage, say something friendly
πείθω	a) persuade, convince, win over, please, assure, reassure; b) be persuaded/convinced, be certain, submit (to), comply, conform to; c) have confidence
πέμπω	send
σπείρω	sow seed
τρεῖς, τρία	three
φέρω	1) bring, conduct, lead, direct; 2) bear, bring, direct, establish; 3) bear; 4) bear, produce

12 Perfect and PluPerfect

12.1 The Perfect Tense

12.1.1 So far we've covered two of the three Greek aspects, simple and continuous. Now, we will learn the third aspect of Greek verbs:

12.1.1.1 *Completive*— reflects upon a complex state of affairs. It can involve past or present time, but is usually translated as past time in a way that affects the speaker's present circumstances (e.g., "Yes, I *have* played basketball.").

12.1.2 The perfect tense stem undergoes *reduplication*.

12.1.2.1 If the verb begins with a consonant, the consonant is reduplicated and the two consonants are divided by an epsilon. Example: λυ → λελυ → λέλυκα (I have released)

12.1.2.2 If the consonant that was reduplicated is one of the three (hard) fricatives φ, χ or θ, it will change to a stop (π, κ, or τ).

    i. φανερόω → φαφανερο → πεφανέρωκα
    ii. χαρίζομαι → χεχαρίζ → κεχάχισμαι
    iii. θεραπεύω → θεθεραπευ → τεθεράπευμαι

  b. If the verb begins with a vowel or diphthong, the vowel will lengthen. For example:
    i. ἀγαπάω → ἠγάπηκα (I have loved)
  c. A *compound verb* reduplicates the verbal part of a compound verb.[1] For example:
    i. ἐκβάλλω → ἐκβέβληκα

---

[1] The same things happen with the augment in the aorist and imperfect tenses: it is only added to the beginning of verb stem (see section 9.1).

12.2 Perfect Active Indicative

12.2.1 The perfect active tense uses the tense formative κα and α. One irregularity, however, is the form of the 3rd singular (see below), which changes to κε. Otherwise, the tense formative and reduplication make the perfect active tense easy to spot.

12.2.1 *Table of Verb Tenses*

Tense	Aug/ Red	Tense stem	TF + CV	Endings	First singular
Present act		pres	o/ε	prim act	λύω
Present mid/pas		pres	o/ε	prim mid/pas	λύομαι
Imperfect act	ε	pres	o/ε	sec act	ἔλυον
Imperfect mid/pas	ε	pres	o/ε	sec mid/pas	ἐλυόμην
Future act		fut act	σ/εσ + o/ε	prim act	λύσω μενῶ
Future mid		fut act	σ/εσ + o/ε	prim mid/pas	πορεύσομαι μενοῦμαι
Future pas		aor pas	θησ/ησ + o/ε	prim mid/pas	λυθήσομαι ἀποσταλήσομαι
Aorist act	ε	aor act	σα/α / o/ε	sec act	ἔλυσα ἔμεινα ἔλαβον
Aorist mid	ε	aor act	σα / o/ε	sec mid/pas	ἐλυσάμην ἐγενόμην
Aorist pas	ε	aor pas	θη/η	sec act	ἐλύθην ἐγράφην
Perfect act	λε		κα/α	prim act	λέλυκα γέγονα
Perfect mid/pas	λε			prim mid/pas	λέλυμαι

12.2.2 Verbal Form of Perfect Active Indicative

| Redup | + | Perfect Active Tense Stem | + | TF | + | Prim Act Ending |

12.2.3 Paradigm of Perfect Active Indicative

	Form	Gloss	Ending
1ˢᵗ Sg	λέλυκα	I have released	
2ⁿᵈ Sg	λέλυκας	You have released	ς
3ʳᵈ Sg	λέλυκε(ν)	He, she, it has released	(ν)
1ˢᵗ Pl	λελύκαμεν	We have released	μεν
2ⁿᵈ Pl	λελύκατε	You (all) have released	τε
3ʳᵈ Pl	λελύκασι(ν)	They have released	σι(ν)

Examples:

ὑμεῖς <u>ἀπεστάλκατε</u> πρὸς Ἰωάννην, καὶ <u>μεμαρτύρηκεν</u> τῇ ἀληθείᾳ·
You <u>have sent</u> to John, and <u>he has testified</u> to the truth.[2]

12.3 Perfect Middle/Passive Indicative

12.3.1 *Table of Verb Tenses*

Tense	Aug/Red	Tense stem	TF + CV	Endings	First singular
Present act		pres	o/ε	prim act	λύω
Present mid/pas		pres	o/ε	prim mid/pas	λύομαι
Imperfect act	ε	pres	o/ε	sec act	ἔλυον
Imperfect mid/pas	ε	pres	o/ε	sec mid/pas	ἐλυόμην
Future act		fut act	σ/εσ + o/ε	prim act	λύσω μενῶ
Future mid		fut act	σ/εσ + o/ε	prim mid/pas	πορεύσομαι μενοῦμαι

---

[2] Jn 5:33.

A Concise Greek Grammar

Future pas		aor pas	θησ/ησ + o/ε	prim mid/pas	λυθήσομαι ἀποσταλήσομαι
Aorist act	ε	aor act	σα/α / o/ε	sec act	ἔλυσα ἔμεινα ἔλαβον
Aorist mid	ε	aor act	σα / o/ε	sec mid/pas	ἐλυσάμην ἐγενόμην
Aorist pas	ε	aor pas	θη/η	sec act	ἐλύθην ἐγράφην
Perfect act	λε		κα/α	prim act	λέλυκα γέγονα
Perfect mid/pas	λε			prim mid/pas	λέλυμαι

12.3.2 Verbal Form of Perfect Middle/Passive Indicative

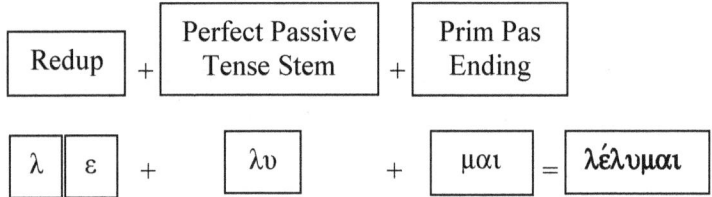

12.3.3 Paradigm of Perfect Middle/Passive Indicative

	Form	Gloss	Ending
1st Sg	λέλυμαι	I have been released	μαι
2nd Sg	λέλυσαι	You have been released	σαι
3rd Sg	λέλυται	He, she, it has been released	ται
1st Pl	λελύμεθα	We have been released	μεθα
2nd Pl	λέλυσθε	You (all) have been released	σθε
3rd Pl	λέλυνται	They have been released	νται

Examples:

ἀλλὰ καθὼς <u>δεδοκιμάσμεθα</u> ὑπὸ τοῦ θεοῦ πιστευθῆναι τὸ εὐαγγέλιον οὕτως λαλοῦμεν, οὐχ ὡς ἀνθρώποις ἀρέσκοντες ἀλλὰ θεῷ τῷ δοκιμάζοντι τὰς καρδίας ἡμῶν.
…but just as <u>we have been approved</u> by God to be entrusted with the gospel, so we speak, not as pleasing men, but God who examines our hearts.[3]

12.4 PluPerfect Indicative

12.4.1 The pluperfect tense is a rare tense[4] used to describe an action that was completed in past time, but the effects are felt *after* the time of the action and *before (or at the time of)* the time of the speaker. For example, "I *had worked* on this grammar for years." The aspect is the same as the perfect tense, so both describe a state resulting from a previous event. The difference is simply *when* the results of the event are felt. Due to its complexity, the pluperfect is sometimes translated as simple past tense (aorist).

12.4.2 The pluperfect is like the aorist and future in that has a "first" and "second" form. The main difference is that the second pluperfect lacks the tense formative.

12.4.3 The plurperfect middle/passive is different, however, in that it does not have a connecting vowel or a tense formative.

12.4.4 The pluperfect has an optional augment in front of the reduplication.

---

[3] 1 Thess 2:4.
[4] According to Wallace, *GGBB*, 583, the pluperfect appears a total of 86 times in the New Testament. However, in my results with Logos, there are 88 occurences (in 86 verses; Acts 19:32 and John 5:17 are the two verses with multiple pluperfect instances).

12.5 12.5 PluPerfect Active Indicative
12.5.1 *Table of Verb Tenses*

Tense	Aug/ Red	Tense stem	TF + CV	Endings	First singular
Present act		pres	o/ε	prim act	λύω
Present mid/pas		pres	o/ε	prim mid/pas	λύομαι
Imperfect act	ε	pres	o/ε	sec act	ἔλυον
Imperfect mid/pas	ε	pres	o/ε	sec mid/pas	ἐλυόμην
Future act		fut act	σ/εσ + o/ε	prim act	λύσω μενῶ
Future mid		fut act	σ/εσ + o/ε	prim mid/pas	πορεύσομαι μενοῦμαι
Future pas		aor pas	θησ/ησ + o/ε	prim mid/pas	λυθήσομαι ἀποσταλήσομαι
Aorist act	ε	aor act	σα/α / o/ε	sec act	ἔλυσα ἔμεινα ἔλαβον
Aorist mid	ε	aor act	σα / o/ε	sec mid/pas	ἐλυσάμην ἐγενόμην
Aorist pas	ε	aor pas	θη/η		sec act	ἐλύθην ἐγράφην
Perfect act	λε		κα/α	prim act	λέλυκα γέγονα
Perfect mid/pas	λε			prim mid/pas	λέλυμαι
Pluperf act	[ε]λε	perf act	κ / ει	sec act	[ε]λελύκειν [ε]γεγράφειν
Pluperf mid/pas	[ε]λε	perf pas		sec pas	[ε]λελύμην

12.5.2 Verbal Form of PluPerfect Active Indicative

| Redup | + | TF (κ) | + | CV (ει) | + | Perfect Tense Stem | + | Sec Act Endings |

| λ | ε | + | κ | + | ει | + | λυ | + | ν |

= λελύκειν

12.5.3 Paradigm of PluPerfect Active Indicative

	First (with TF)	Second (no TF)	Ending
1st Sg	(ἐ)λελύκειν	(ἐ)γεγράφειν	ν
2nd Sg	(ἐ)λελύκεις	(ἐ)γεγράφεις	ς
3rd Sg	(ἐ)λελύκει(ν)	(ἐ)γεγράφει(ν)	
1st Pl	(ἐ)λελύκειμεν	(ἐ)γεγράφειμεν	μεν
2nd Pl	(ἐ)λελύκειτε	(ἐ)γεγράφειτε	τε
3rd Pl	(ἐ)λελύκεισαν	(ἐ)γεγράφεισαν	σαν

Examples:

εἰ δὲ ἐγνώκειτε τί ἐστιν, Ἔλεος θέλω καὶ οὐ θυσίαν, οὐκ ἂν κατεδικάσατε τοὺς ἀναιτίους.
But if you had known what this means, 'I desire mercy and not sacrifice,' you would not have condemned the guiltless.[5]

ὡς δὲ ἐγεύσατο ὁ ἀρχιτρίκλινος τὸ ὕδωρ οἶνον γεγενημένον, καὶ οὐκ ᾔδει πόθεν ἐστίν, οἱ δὲ διάκονοι ᾔδεισαν οἱ ἠντληκότες τὸ ὕδωρ, φωνεῖ τὸν νυμφίον ὁ ἀρχιτρίκλινος…
When the steward tasted the water that had become wine, and did not know where it [had] came from (though the servants who had drawn the water knew), the steward called the bridegroom…[6]

---

[5] Mt 12:7.
[6] Jn 2:9.

12.6 PlurPerfect Middle/Passive
12.6.1 *Table of Verb Tenses*

Tense	Aug/ Red	Tense stem	TF + CV	Endings	First singular
Present act		pres	o/ε	prim act	λύω
Present mid/pas		pres	o/ε	prim mid/pas	λύομαι
Imperfect act	ε	pres	o/ε	sec act	ἔλυον
Imperfect mid/pas	ε	pres	o/ε	sec mid/pas	ἐλυόμην
Future act		fut act	σ/εσ + o/ε	prim act	λύσω / μενῶ
Future mid		fut act	σ/εσ + o/ε	prim mid/pas	πορεύσομαι / μενοῦμαι
Future pas		aor pas	θησ/ησ + o/ε	prim mid/pas	λυθήσομαι / ἀποσταλήσομαι
Aorist act	ε	aor act	σα/α / o/ε	sec act	ἔλυσα / ἔμεινα / ἔλαβον
Aorist mid	ε	aor act	σα / o/ε	sec mid/pas	ἐλυσάμην / ἐγενόμην
Aorist pas	ε	aor pas	θη/η	sec act	ἐλύθην / ἐγράφην
Perfect act	λε		κα/α	prim act	λέλυκα / γέγονα
Perfect mid/pas	λε			prim mid/pas	λέλυμαι
Pluperf act	[ε]λε	perf act	κ / ει	sec act	[ἐ]λελύκειν / [ἐ]γεγράφειν
Pluperf mid/pas	[ε]λε	perf pas		sec pas	[ἐ]λελύμην

12.6.2 Verbal Form of PluPerfect Middle/Passive

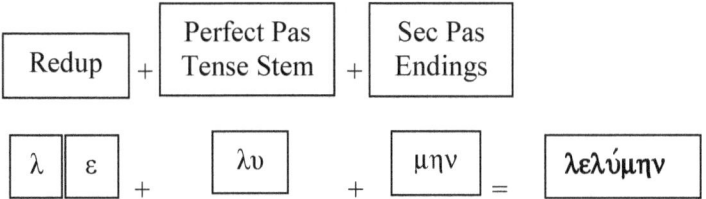

12.6.3 Paradigm of PluPerfect Middle/Passive Indicative

	Form	Gloss	CV	Ending
1st Sg	(ἐ)λελύμην	I had been destroyed		μην
2nd Sg	(ἐ)λελυσο	You had been destroyed		σο
3rd Sg	(ἐ)λελυτο	He/she/it had been destroyed		το
1st Pl	(ἐ)λελύμεθα	We had been destroyed		μεθα
2nd Pl	(ἐ)λελυσθε	You (all) had been destroyed		σθε
3rd Pl	(ἐ)λελυντο	They had been destroyed		ντο

Examples:

ταῦτα εἶπαν οἱ γονεῖς αὐτοῦ ὅτι ἐφοβοῦντο τοὺς Ἰουδαίους· ἤδη γὰρ <u>συνετέθειντο</u> [mid] οἱ Ἰουδαῖοι ἵνα ἐάν τις αὐτὸν ὁμολογήσῃ Χριστόν, ἀποσυνάγωγος γένηται.

His parents said this because they were afraid of the Jews; for the Jews <u>had already agreed</u> that if anyone confessed Him to be Christ, he was to be put out of the synagogue.[7]

---

[7] Jn 9:22.

καὶ κατέβη ἡ βροχὴ καὶ ἦλθον οἱ ποταμοὶ καὶ ἔπνευσαν οἱ ἄνεμοι καὶ προσέπεσαν τῇ οἰκίᾳ ἐκείνῃ, καὶ οὐκ ἔπεσεν, <u>τεθεμελίωτο</u> [pas] γὰρ ἐπὶ τὴν πέτραν.[8]

"And the rain fell, and the floods came, and the winds blew and slammed against that house; and yet it did not fall, for it <u>had</u> <u>been</u> <u>founded</u> on the rock.

Vocabulary

λίθος, -ου, ὁ	stone
μηδέ	a) and not, nor; b) don't even
πρεσβύτερος, -ου, ὁ	1) older, the older one, elders, ancestors; 2) elders
τιοῦτος, -αύτη, -οῦτον	such, such as this

---

[8] Mt 7:25.

Chapter Thirteen: Subjunctive and Infinitive

13 Subjunctive and Infinitive

13.1 Introduction to Non-Indicative Moods

13.1.1 So far, all the verbs that we have discussed have been in the indicative mood, which make a statement or ask a simple question. The author asserts the plain reality of the verbal event. We now move onto a number of non-indicative moods.

13.1.2 As Porter puts it, "Nonindicative moods (subjunctive, optative, imperative) indicate the 'projection' of a verbal event according to the mind or view of the speaker or writer. In other words, by using a nonindicative mood, the author creates a 'possible' world or state of affairs."[1]

13.2 Subjunctive Mood

13.2.1 The subjunctive mood, however, is primarily used to express a probability. At times it can be used for possibility and hypothetical possibility.[2] Example: "I *may go swimming* today" and "*if* Jessica *finds out*, the surprise will be ruined." As you can see, the words "if," "may," and "might" are often used in translating the subjunctive (though these key terms need not always be used).

13.2.2 Subjunctive verbs have no time significance, only aspect. As we have already learned, "present tense" and present tense stems have a continuous aspect while "aorist tense" and aorist tense stems exhibit a simple aspect. There is no future subjunctive. Examples:

---

[1] Porter et. al., *Fundamentals*, 155.
[2] This is the function of the "optative" mood, which was largely replaced by the subjunctive in the NT period (there are less than 70 optatives in the NT).

Present: ἀγάπην δὲ μὴ ἔχω, οὐδὲν ὠφελοῦμαι.
"But if I am not having love, I gain nothing."[3]

Aorist: Διδάσκαλε, τί ἀγαθὸν ποιήσω ἵνα σχῶ ζωὴν αἰώνιον;
"Teacher, what good thing might I do in order to have eternal life?"[4] (Hübner)

13.2.3 As seen in the aorist example above, subjunctive verbs are often used in conditional statements with ἵνα and ἐάν clauses.

13.2.4 In conditional statements like "if I am not having love, then I gain nothing" the "if" clause is called the *protasis* (since it typically comes first), and the "then" clause is called the *apodosis* (since it comes after).[5] Sometimes the order is reversed.[6] The important thing to remember is that the *contingency* is always attached to protasis, regardless of where it falls in a sentence.

13.2.5 Subjunctive verbs are easy to identify because they all use the connecting vowels ω or η, and they all use the primary verb endings.

13.3 Present Subjunctive

13.3.1 The present subjunctive indicates a continuous probability or possibility. Example: Κύριε, ἐὰν θέλῃς ("Lord, if you are willing...").[7]

---

[3] 1 Cor 13:3.
[4] Mt 19:16.
[5] For a discussion of conditional sentences, see Wallace, *GGBB*, 682.
[6] E.g., Mt 4:9; Mk 14:21, etc.
[7] Mt 8:2.

13.3.2 *Table of Subjunctive Verb Tenses*

Tense	Tense stem	TF + CV	Endings	First singular
Present act	pres	ω/η	prim act	λύω
Present mid/pas	pres	ω/η	prim mid/pas	λύωμαι
Aorist act	aor act	σ(ω) + ω/η	prim act	λύσω / λάβω
Aorist mid	aor act	σ(ω) + ω/η	prim mid/pas	λύσωμαι / γένωμαι
Aorist pas	aor pas	θη + ω/η	prim act	λυθῶ / γραφῶ

13.3.3 Verbal Form of Present Subjunctive

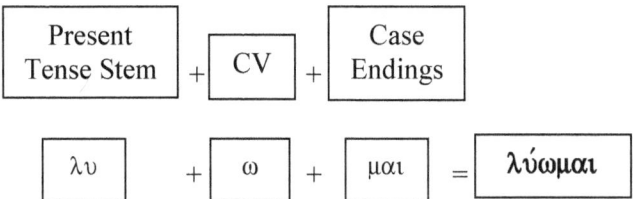

Examples:

Ἐὰν ταῖς γλώσσαις τῶν ἀνθρώπων <u>λαλῶ</u> καὶ τῶν ἀγγέλων, ἀγάπην δὲ μὴ ἔχω, γέγονα χαλκὸς ἠχῶν ἢ κύμβαλον ἀλαλάζον. καὶ ἐὰν <u>ἔχω</u> προφητείαν καὶ εἰδῶ τὰ μυστήρια πάντα καὶ πᾶσαν τὴν γνῶσιν καὶ ἐὰν <u>ἔχω</u> πᾶσαν τὴν πίστιν ὥστε ὄρη μεθιστάναι, ἀγάπην δὲ μὴ <u>ἔχω</u>, οὐθέν εἰμι. κἂν <u>ψωμίσω</u> πάντα τὰ ὑπάρχοντά μου καὶ ἐὰν <u>παραδῶ</u> τὸ σῶμά μου ἵνα καυχήσωμαι, ἀγάπην δὲ μὴ <u>ἔχω</u>, οὐδὲν ὠφελοῦμαι.
<u>If</u> in the tongues of people and of angels <u>I am speaking</u>, but have not love, I am a noisy gong or a clanging cymbal. And <u>if I am having</u> prophetic powers and understand all mysteries and all knowledge, and <u>if</u> <u>I am having</u> all faith, so as to remove mountains, but <u>am having</u> not love,

I am nothing. If I am giving away all I have, and if I am delivering up my body to be burned, but am having not love, I gain nothing.[8] (Hübner)

13.4 Aorist Subjunctive

13.4.1 The aorist subjunctive indicates a simple probability or possibility. Example: ἐὰν δὲ ἐρωτήσω, οὐ μὴ ἀποκριθῆτε. ("If I tell you, you will not believe.")[9]

13.4.2 *Table of Subjunctive Verb Tenses*

Tense	Tense stem	TF + CV	Endings	First singular
Present act	pres	ω/η	prim act	λύω
Present mid/pas	pres	ω/η	prim mid/pas	λύωμαι
Aorist act	aor act	σ(α) /+/ ω/η	prim act	λύσω λάβω
Aorist mid	aor act	σ(α) /+/ ω/η	prim mid/pas	λύσωμαι γένωμαι
Aorist pas	aor pas	θη /+/ ω/η	prim act	λυθῶ γράφω

13.4.3 Verbal Form of Aorist Subjunctive

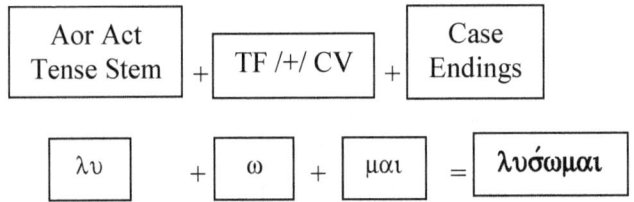

Example:
τοίνυν ἐξερχώμεθα πρὸς αὐτὸν ἔξω τῆς παρεμβολῆς τὸν ὀνειδισμὸν αὐτοῦ φέροντες.
So, let us go out to him outside the camp, bearing his reproach.[10]

---

[8] 1 Cor 13:1-3.
[9] Lk 22:68.

13.4.4 Table of εἰμί Verbs (Complete)

	Imperfect	Present	Future	Subjunctive
1 sg	ἤμην	εἰμί	ἔσομαι	ὦ
2 sg	ἦς, ἦσθα	εἶ	ἔσῃ	ᾖς
3 sg	ἦν	ἐστί(ν)	ἔσται	ᾖ
1 pl	ἦμεν, ἤμεθα	ἐσμέν	ἐσόμεθα	ὦμεν
2 pl	ἦτε	ἐστέ	ἔσεσθε	ἦτε
3 pl	ἦσαν	εἰσί(ν)	ἔσονται	ὦσι(ν)

Example:
καὶ εἶπεν Ὅταν μαιοῦσθε τὰς Εβραίας καὶ <u>ὦσιν</u> πρὸς τῷ τίκτειν, ἐὰν μὲν ἄρσεν <u>ᾖ</u>, ἀποκτείνατε αὐτό, ἐὰν δὲ θῆλυ, περιποιεῖσθε αὐτό.
And he said, 'Whenever you act as midwives to the Hebrew women and <u>they should be</u> at the birthing stage, <u>if</u> then <u>it be</u> male, kill it, but if female, preserve it alive.[11] (NETS)

13.5 Infinitive

13.5.1 The infinitive is an indeclinable verbal noun that stands outside of the indicative mood. It is less connected with the surrounding context, so it is less inflected and overlaps with the uses of both the verb and the noun.

13.5.2 In English, the infinitive can be rendered with "to" before it, although it sometimes is not necessary.

Example: "<u>To watch</u> TV is a waste of time, but <u>to read</u> books is time well spent."

Example: "What do you do on weekends? <u>Walk</u>? <u>Ride bike</u>? <u>Read</u>?"

13.5.3 Like a verb, the infinitive has tense and voice, but not person or number. It can have an object and be modified by adverbs.

---

[10] Hb 13:13.
[11] Ex 1:16, LXX.

13.5.4 Like a noun, the infinitive can function as a noun, being articular and anarthrous, the object of a preposition, or be modified by an adjective.

13.5.5 **Present Infinitive**

13.5.5.1 *Table of Infinitive Tenses*

Tense	Ending
Present act	ειν
Present mid/pas	εσθαι
Aorist act	σαι/ειν
Aorist mid	σασθαι/εσθαι
Aorist pas	θηναι/ηναι

13.5.5.2 **Verbal Form of Present Infinitive**

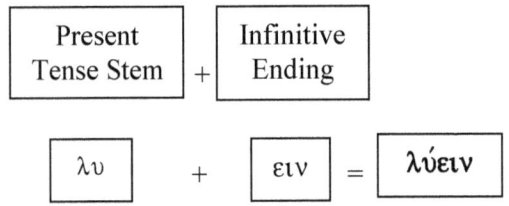

Example:

ἵνα δυνατὸς ᾖ καὶ <u>παρακαλεῖν</u> ἐν τῇ διδασκαλίᾳ τῇ ὑγιαινούσῃ καὶ τοὺς ἀντιλέγοντας ἐλέγχειν.
...so that he will be able both <u>to be exhorting</u> in sound doctrine and to be refuting those who contradict.[12] (Hübner)

ὁ θεὸς Ἀβραὰμ καὶ [ὁ θεὸς] Ἰσαὰκ καὶ [ὁ θεὸς] Ἰακώβ, ὁ θεὸς τῶν πατέρων ἡμῶν, ἐδόξασεν τὸν παῖδα αὐτοῦ Ἰησοῦν, ὃν ὑμεῖς μὲν παρεδώκατε καὶ ἠρνήσασθε κατὰ πρόσωπον Πιλάτου, κρίναντος ἐκείνου <u>ἀπολύειν</u>·

---

[12] Mk 5:10.

"The God of Abraham, Isaac and Jacob, the God of our fathers, has glorified his servant Jesus, the one whom you have delivered and disowned in the presence of Pilate, when he had decided <u>to release</u> him.[13] (Hübner)

13.5.6 Aorist Infinitive

13.5.6.1 *Table of Infinitive Tenses*

Tense	Ending
Present act	ειν
Present mid/pas	εσθαι
Aorist act	σαι/ειν
Aorist mid	σασθαι/εσθαι
Aorist pas	θηναι/ηναι
Perfect act	κεναι
Perfect mid/pas	σθαι

13.6 Verbal Form of Aorist Infinitive

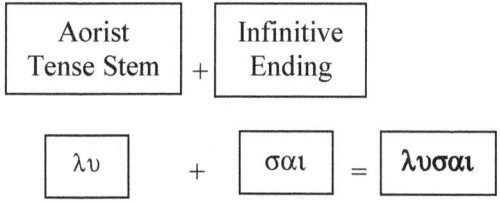

Example:

Ὀψὲ δὲ σαββάτων, τῇ ἐπιφωσκούσῃ εἰς μίαν σαββάτων ἦλθεν Μαριὰμ ἡ Μαγδαληνὴ καὶ ἡ ἄλλη Μαρία <u>θεωρῆσαι</u> τὸν τάφον.
Now after the Sabbath, as it began to dawn toward the first day of the week, Mary Magdalene and the other Mary came <u>to look</u> at the grave.[14]

---

[13] Acts 3:13.
[14] Mt 28:1.

13.6.1 Perfect Infinitive

13.6.1.1 *Table of Infinitive Tenses*

Tense	Ending
Present act	ειν
Present mid/pas	εσθαι
Aorist act	σαι/ειν
Aorist mid	σασθαι/εσθαι
Aorist pas	θηναι/ηναι
Perfect act	κεναι
Perfect mid/pas	σθαι

13.6.1.2 Verbal Form of Perfect Infinitive

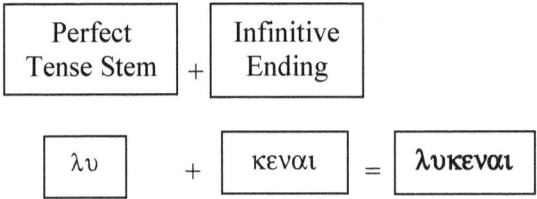

Example:

ἀρκετὸς γὰρ ὁ παρεληλυθὼς χρόνος τὸ βούλημα τῶν ἐθνῶν <u>κατειργάσθαι</u> πεπορευμένους ἐν ἀσελγείαις, ἐπιθυμίαις, οἰνοφλυγίαις, κώμοις, πότοις καὶ ἀθεμίτοις εἰδωλολατρίαις.[15]

For the time already past is sufficient for you <u>to have carried out</u> the desire of the Gentiles, having pursued a course of sensuality, lusts, drunkenness, carousing, drinking parties and abominable idolatries.

---

[15] 1 Pt 4:3.

Vocabulary

δίκαιος, -α, -ον	upright, just
μέλλω	a) be in the offing, be about (to), being going (to), (in the) future, to come; b) have in mind, intend, plan (on), to delay
ἀπόλλυμι	1) destroy, ruin, kill, destroy; 2) lose, perish
ἀπολύω	1) release, deliver, free; 2) send off, dismiss; 4) go off, leave
εἴτε	If…(or) if, whether…or

14 Imperative and -μι Verbs

14.1 Imperative

14.1.1 In contrast to the indicative mood (which asserts) and subjunctive mood (which suggests a probability), the imperative mood makes a command.

14.1.2 The imperative has no time significance, but it can exist in either the present or aorist tenses, having continuous and simple aspects respectively. Below are some examples in English:

Present: "Be searching!" or "Keep on searching!"

Aorist: "Search!"

14.1.3 The imperative can also exist in second and third person forms:

Second: "You search!"

Third: "Let her search!" or "She must search!"

14.1.4 The imperative reflects the indicative mood in that it uses the same connecting vowel and tense formatives. Thus, the present tense imperative uses the connecting vowel ο/ε, and the aorist imperative uses either the connecting vowel (ο/ε) or tense formatives (σα/θη/η).

14.1.5 For endings, the imperative uses a unique (and unusually patterned) set of morphemes that set it apart from the subjunctive and infinitive.

Chapter Fourteen: Imperative and –μι Verbs

14.1.6 *Table of Imperative Morphemes*

	All Active and Aorist Passive	Middle/Passive
2nd Sg	?	?
3rd Sg	τω	σθω
2nd Pl	τε	σθε
3rd Pl	τωσαν	σθωσαν

14.1.7 Note the overlap with the indicative in the 2nd person plural. Context will usually determine if the imperative is being used.[1]

14.1.8 Note also the question mark for the 2nd singular. This means there is no known pattern. In these cases, the ending may be an indicative personal ending (like ν), or something else.

14.1.9 Verbal Form of Present Imperative

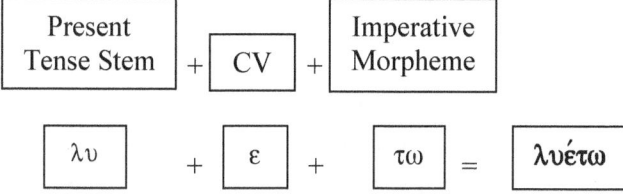

Examples:

εἰς ἣν δ' ἂν εἰσέλθητε οἰκίαν, πρῶτον <u>λέγετε</u>, Εἰρήνη τῷ οἴκῳ τούτῳ.
And whatever house you all enter, first <u>say</u>, 'Peace be in this house!'[2] (Hübner)

εἴ τις ἔχει ὦτα ἀκούειν <u>ἀκουέτω</u>.
If anyone has ears to hear, <u>hear</u>![3] (Hübner)

---

[1] See Mk 11:22 and Jn 14:1-2 for difficult cases.
[2] Lk 10:5.
[3] Mk 4:23.

14.1.10 Verbal Form of Aorist Imperative

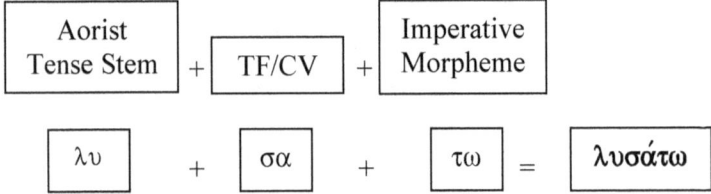

Examples:

οἱ δὲ δαίμονες παρεκάλουν αὐτὸν λέγοντες, Εἰ ἐκβάλλεις ἡμᾶς, <u>ἀπόστειλον</u> ἡμᾶς εἰς τὴν ἀγέλην τῶν χοίρων.
And the demons begged him, saying, "If you cast us out, <u>send</u> us away into the herd of pigs."[4] (Hübner)

καὶ προσῆλθεν ὁ Ἰησοῦς καὶ ἁψάμενος αὐτῶν εἶπεν, <u>Ἐγέρθητε</u> καὶ μὴ φοβεῖσθε.
But Jesus came and touched them, saying, "<u>Rise</u>, and have no fear."[5]

14.2 -μι Verbs

14.2.1 As you have learned so far, most Greek verbs end in an omicron which then lengthens into an omega. Instead of ending in -ω, -μι verbs end in μι. For example, compare the two lexical words δοκέ<u>ω</u> ("I think") with δίδω<u>μι</u> ("I give").

14.2.2 The forms of -μι verbs match regular verbs except for the present, imperfect, and second aorist tenses. In those cases, several of the previous verbal rules you've learned come to converge into some unusual forms. For example, the present tense forms of -μι verbs change in three noticeable ways:

14.2.2.1 The initial stem letter is reduplicated, separated by an iota. Example: δο → <u>δι</u>δο → διδω → δίδωμι

14.2.2.2 Connecting vowels are usually absent.[6] Example: δίδ<u>οτε</u>.

---

[4] Mt 8:31. The usage here is a present imperative.
[5] Mt 17:7. The usage here is an aorist passive imperative. What does Danker in *CL* say about the passive use of this verb?

Chapter Fourteen: Imperative and –μι Verbs

14.2.2.3 In addition to the active first person verb ending -μι, the third person endings are changed from ι (sg) and νσι (pl) to σι (sg) and ασι (pl). Example: δίδο<u>ασι</u> ("they are giving").

14.2.3 *Table of Active Indicative -μι Verbs*

	Present	Imperfect	Future	Aorist	Perfect
1st Sg	δίδωμι	ἐδίδουν	δώσω	ἔδωκα	δέδωκα
2nd Sg	δίδως	ἐδίδους	δώσεις	ἔδωκας	δέδωκας
3rd Sg	δίδωσι(ν)	ἐδίδου	δώσει	ἔδωκε(ν)	δέδωκε(ν)
1st Pl	δίδομεν	ἐδίδομεν	δώσομεν	ἐδώκαμεν	δεδώκαμεν
2nd Pl	δίδοτε	ἐδίδοτε	δώσετε	ἐδώκατε	δεδώκατε
3rd Pl	διδόασι(ν)	ἐδίδουν	δώσουσι(ν)	ἔδωκαν	δέδωκαν

14.2.4 κα is usually used as a tense formative for the aorist endings (instead of the perfect). Example: ἔδω<u>κα</u> ("I gave").

14.2.5 There are many more unusual forms of -μι verbs, but the above rules will provide clear direction for the majority of cases. Don't worry about memorizing all the forms of these verbs, since there are only a handful of common –μι verbs in the New Testament.

---

[6] The connecting vowel is used in -μι verbs in the imperfect singular and future.

Vocabulary

λοιπός, -ή, -όν	1) remaining; 2) other, rest (of); 3) from now on, henceforth, at last, from now on, in the future, otherwise, furthermore, finally
Μωϋσῆς, -έως, ὁ	Moses
παραδίδωμι	hand over
πίπτω	a) fall, collapse, fall; b) fall (down); c) fall/perish; d) fall
ὑπάρχω	1) be there, take place, have place, be at (one's disposal, belong (to), property, holdings; 2) be
ἀνίστημι	1) raise up; b) rise (up), get up
δίδωμι	give
ἔθνος, -ους, τό	1) people (group); 2) non-Israelite persons, Gentiles

15 Introduction to Participles and Present Participles

15.1 Introduction to Participles

15.1.1 What happens when you mix a verb and an adjective in a blender? You make a participle! Participles are a challenging part of learning Greek because they are so flexible in their usage. They can behave as nouns, adverbs, adjectives, and verbs. They are technically called "declinable verbal adjectives."[1] All that means is that the participle has two sides to it: the adjective side (where it derives its gender, number, and case), and the verbal side (where it derives its tense and voice). The closest thing to a participle in English is an "ing" word like "sleeping" or "studying."

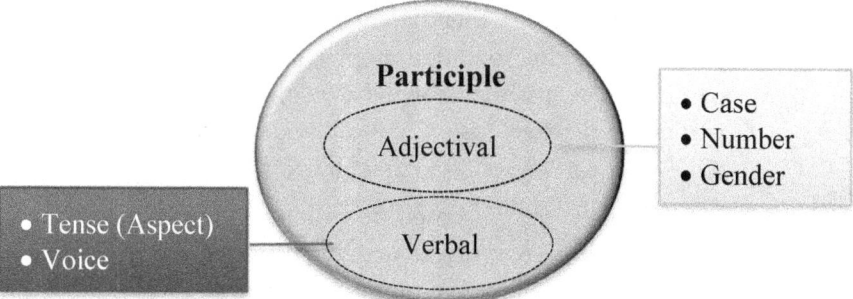

---

[1] Wallace, *GGBB*, 613.

15.1.2 To help wrap your mind around participles, note how the word "singing" can be used in English:

15.1.2.1 "I was *singing*." (verbial—functioning as a verb)

15.1.2.2 "I tripped *while singing*." (adverbial—functioning as an adverb; it modifies a verb)

15.1.2.3 "The *singing* man woke up his wife." (adjectival—functioning as an adjective; it modifies a noun)

15.1.2.4 "The *singing* woke up his wife." (substantival—substituting/functioning as a noun)[2]

15.1.3 As indicated in the graphic above, there are two basic functions of Greek participles:

15.1.3.1 **Adverbial Participles** — The participle functions as an *adverb* by modifying a verb or verbal phrase. For example, "Jessica snored while sleeping." The participle "sleeping" is telling something about the verb "snored." Adverbial participles are anarthrous (they don't use the article).

15.1.3.2 **Adjectival Participles** — The participle usually functions as an *adjective* by modifying a noun or noun phrase. For example, "Jessica, texting her friend during class, is not studying." The participle "texting" is modifying the noun "Jessica." Adjectival participles are articular (use the article). Translating adjectival participles is often loose, and pronouns may need to be added. Adjectival participles also come in two flavors:

15.1.3.2.1 *Attributive Participle*: modifies a noun or noun phrase just like an adjective. It agrees with the word it modifies in case, number, and gender. Example: ὁ ἄνθρωπος ὁ λέγων τῷ ὄχλῳ ἐστίν ὁ διδάσκαλός μου — "the man speaking to the crowd is my teacher."

15.1.3.2.2 *Substantival Participle*: functions like a noun. Case is determined by function in the sentence, while number and gender are determined by what or who the participle is

---

[2] This is the equivalent of a *gerund* in English grammar.

representing. Example: ὁ τῷ ὄχλῳ λέγων ἐστίν ὁ διδάσκαλός μου — "the <u>one who is speaking</u> to the crowd is my teacher."

15.1.4 To make things more complicated, both adverbial and adjectival participles have the same form, so it is sometimes debatable how they are being used.

15.1.5 The basic features of participles are shown through a single set of morphemes. These morphemes show the voice, gender, and declension of a participle at the same time.

15.1.5.1 *Table of Participle Morphemes*

	Masculine	Feminine	Neuter
active	ντ (3)	ουσα (1)	ντ (3)
mid/pas	μενο (2)	μενη (1)	μενο (2)

15.2 Present (Continuous) Participles

15.2.1 The present participle describes a continuous action.

15.2.2 The present participle is always adverbial, which means it always modifies a verb.

15.2.3 Therefore, it must agree with the noun or pronoun it is modifying in case, number, and gender.

15.2.4 Since it describes a continuous action, translation of present participles may require the keywords "while" or "because." For example: <u>Περιπατῶν</u> δὲ παρὰ τὴν θάλασσαν τῆς Γαλιλαίας εἶδεν δύο ἀδελφούς is translated "<u>while walking</u> by the Sea of Galilee, he saw two brothers."[3] The participle "while walking" modifies the verb "he saw."

---

[3] Mt 4:18.

15.3 Present Active Participle
15.3.1 Table of Participle Tenses

Tense	Aug/ Red	Tense stem	TF + CV	Morpheme
Present act		pres	o	ντ/ουσα
Present mid/pas		pres	o	μενο/μενη

15.3.2 Form of the Present Participle

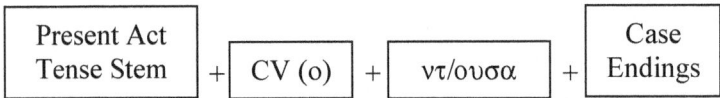

15.3.3 Present Active Participle Paradigm

	Masc	Fem	Neut
Sg Nom	λύων	λύουσα	λῦον
Sg Gen	λύοντος	λυούσης	λύοντος
Sg Dat	λύοντι	λυούσῃ	λύοντι
Sg Acc	λύοντα	λύουσαν	λῦον
Pl Nom	λύοντες	λύουσαι	λύοντα
Pl Gen	λυόντων	λυουσῶν	λυόντων
Pl Dat	λύουσι(ν)	λυούσαις	λύουσι(ν)
Pl Acc	λύοντας	λυούσας	λύοντα

Examples:

Καὶ <u>ἔτι</u> <u>αὐτοῦ</u> <u>λαλοῦντος</u> ἰδοὺ Ἰούδας εἷς τῶν δώδεκα ἦλθεν καὶ μετ' αὐτοῦ ὄχλος πολὺς μετὰ μαχαιρῶν καὶ ξύλων...
<u>While</u> <u>he</u> <u>was</u> <u>still</u> <u>speaking</u>, Judas, one of the twelve, arrived; with him was a large crowd with swords and clubs...[4]

---

[4] Mt 26:47.

Chapter Fifteen: Intro to Participles and Present Participles

15.3.4 Present Active Participle for εἰμί ("being")

	M	F	N
Sg Nom	ὤν	οὖσα	ὄν
Sg Gen	ὄντος	οὔσης	ὄντος
Sg Dat	ὄντι	οὔσῃ	ὄντι
Sg Acc	ὄντα	οὖσαν	ὄν
Pl Nom	ὄντες	οὖσαι	ὄντα
Pl Gen	ὄντων	οὐσῶν	ὄντων
Pl Dat	οὖσι(ν)	οὔσαις	οὖσι(ν)
Pl Acc	ὄντας	οὔσας	ὄντα

15.4 Present Middle/Passive Participle

15.4.1 Table of Participle Tenses

Tense	Aug/ Red	Tense stem	TF + CV	Morpheme
Present act		pres	o	ντ/ουσα
Present mid/pas		pres	o	μενο/μενη

15.4.2 Form of the Present Participle

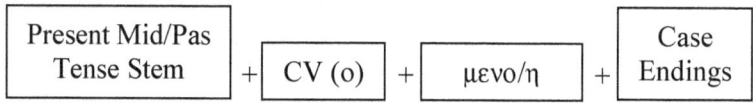

Present Mid/Pas Tense Stem + CV (o) + μενο/η + Case Endings

15.4.3 Present Middle/Passive Participle Paradigm

	M	F	N
Sg Nom	λυόμενος	λυομένη	λυόμενον
Sg Gen	λυομένου	λυομένης	λυομένου
Sg Dat	λυομένῳ	λυομένῃ	λυομένῳ
Sg Acc	λυόμενον	λυομένην	λυόμενον
Pl Nom	λυόμενοι	λυόμεναι	λυόμενα
Pl Gen	λυομένων	λυομένων	λυομένων
Pl Dat	λυομένοις	λυομέναις	λυομένοις
Pl Acc	λυομένους	λυομένας	λυόμενα

Examples:

Εἰσελθὼν δὲ εἰς τὴν συναγωγὴν ἐπαρρησιάζετο ἐπὶ μῆνας τρεῖς <u>διαλεγόμενος</u> <u>καὶ</u> <u>πείθων</u> τὰ περὶ τῆς βασιλείας τοῦ θεοῦ.
And he entered the synagogue and continued speaking out boldly for three months, <u>reasoning and persuading</u> them about the kingdom of God.[5]

Νυνὶ δὲ χωρὶς νόμου δικαιοσύνη θεοῦ πεφανέρωται, <u>μαρτυρουμένη</u> ὑπὸ τοῦ νόμου καὶ τῶν προφητῶν.
But now, apart from the law, the righteousness of God has been disclosed, and is <u>[being] attested</u> by the law and the prophets.[6]

---

[5] Acts 19:8
[6] Rom 3:21.

16 Aorist Participles

16.1 Aorist Participles

16.1.1 Aorist participles indicate an action viewed as a simple whole. Translation usually includes the word "after." Example: λύσας means "after he destroyed."

16.1.2 Aorist participles use the Morpheme ντ in the active and passive, and μεν in the middle.

16.1.3 Like verbs,[1] the only difference between the "First" and "Second" participles is that the First participles use the tense formative, while the Second participles use the connecting vowel (For the sake of simplicity, we will therefore combine the first and second participles in this chapter of the grammar. Nevertheless, I will provide the paradigm to the first participle to provide examples.)

16.2 Aorist Active Participle

16.2.1 Table of Participle Tenses

Tense	Aug/ Red	Tense stem	TF + CV	Morpheme
Present act		pres	o	ντ/ουσα
Present mid/pas		pres	o	μενο/μενη
Aorist act		aor act	σα / o	ντ/σα
Aorist mid		aor act	σα / o	μενο/μενη
Aorist pas		aor pas	θε / ε	ντ/ισα
Perfect act	κε	perf act	κα	οτ/υια
Perfect mid/pas	κε	perf pas		μενο/μενη

---

[1] The exception, of course, is the 2nd Aorist Passive, which (oddly) uses a tense formative instead of a connecting vowel.

16.2.2 Form of Aorist Active Participle

| Aorist Tense Stem | + | TF/CV | + | ντ/σα | + | Case Endings |

16.2.3 (1ˢᵗ) Aorist Active Participle Paradigm

	M	F	N
Sg Nom	λύσας	λύσασα	λῦσαν
Sg Gen	λύσαντος	λυσάσης	λύσαντος
Sg Dat	λύσαντι	λυσάσῃ	λύσαντι
Sg Acc	λύσαντα	λύσασαν	λῦσαν
Pl Nom	λύσαντες	λύσασαι	λύσαντα
Pl Gen	λυσάντων	λυσασῶν	λυσάντων
Pl Dat	λύσασι[ν]	λυσάσαις	λύσασι[ν]
Pl Acc	λύσαντας	λυσάσας	λύσαντα

Examples:

Τί ποιεῖτε λύοντες τὸν πῶλον;
What are you doing, <u>untying</u> the colt?[2]

ὅθεν οἵ τε φίλοι καὶ σωματοφύλακες ὀξεῖαν <u>ἰδόντες</u> τὴν καταλαβοῦσαν αὐτὸν εὔθυναν φοβούμενοι μὴ καὶ τὸ ζῆν ἐκλείπῃ…[3]
Then both friends and bodyguards, <u>seeing</u> the severe punishment that had overtaken him, and fearing that he would lose his life…

---

[2] Mk 11:5.
[3] 3 Mac 2:23.

16.3 Aorist Middle Participle
16.3.1 Table of Participle Tenses

Tense	Aug/ Red	Tense stem	TF + CV	Morpheme
Present act		pres	o	ντ/ουσα
Present mid/pas		pres	o	μενο/μενη
Aorist act		aor act	σα / o	ντ/σα
Aorist mid		aor act	σα / o	μενο/μενη
Aorist pas		aor pas	θε / ε	ντ/ισα
Perfect act	κε	perf act	κα	οτ/υια
Perfect mid/pas	κε	perf pas		μενο/μενη

16.3.2 Form of Aorist Middle Participle

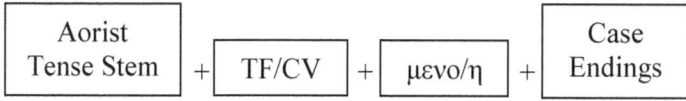

16.3.3 (1ˢᵗ) Aorist Middle Participle Paradigm

	M	F	N
Sg Nom	λυσάμενος	λυσαμένη	λυσάμενον
Sg Gen	λυσαμένου	λυσαμένης	λυσαμένου
Sg Dat	λυσαμένῳ	λυσαμένῃ	λυσαμένῳ
Sg Acc	λυσάμενον	λυσαμένην	λυσάμενον
Pl Nom	λυσάμενοι	λυσάμεναι	λυσάμενα
Pl Gen	λυσαμένων	λυσαμένων	λυσαμένων
Pl Dat	λυσαμένοις	λυσαμέναις	λυσαμένοις
Pl Acc	λυσαμένους	λυσαμένας	λυσάμενα

Examples:

Καὶ προσκαλεσάμενος πάλιν τὸν ὄχλον ἔλεγεν αὐτοῖς, Ἀκούσατέ μου πάντες καὶ σύνετε.
After He called the crown to Him again, He began saying to them, "Listen to Me, all of you, and understand." (Mark 7:14)

16.4 Aorist Passive Participle

16.4.1 Table of Participle Tenses

Tense	Aug/Red	Tense stem	TF + CV	Morpheme
Present act		pres	o	ντ/ουσα
Present mid/pas		pres	o	μενο/μενη
Aorist act		aor act	σα / o	ντ/σα
Aorist mid		aor act	σα / o	μενο/μενη
Aorist pas		aor pas	θε / ε	ντ/ισα
Perfect act	λε	perf act	κα	οτ/υια
Perfect mid/pas	λε	perf pas		μενο/μενη

16.4.2 Form of Aorist Passive Participle

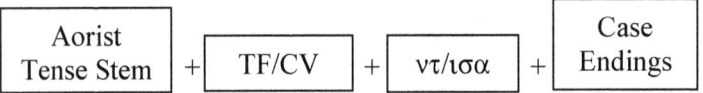

16.4.3 (1ˢᵗ) Aorist Passive Participle Paradigm

	M	F	N
Sg Nom	λυθείς	λυθεῖσα	λυθέν
Sg Gen	λυθέντος	λυθείσης	λυθέντος
Sg Dat	λυθέντι	λυθείσῃ	λυθέντι
Sg Acc	λυθέντα	λυθεῖσαν	λυθέν
Pl Nom	λυθέντες	λυθεῖσαι	λυθέντα
Pl Gen	λυθέντων	λυθεισῶν	λυθέντων
Pl Dat	λυθεῖσι[ν]	λυθείσαις	λυθεῖσι[ν]
Pl Acc	λυθέντας	λυθείσας	λυθέντα

Examples:

βαπτισθεὶς δὲ ὁ Ἰησοῦς εὐθὺς ἀνέβη ἀπὸ τοῦ ὕδατος· καὶ ἰδοὺ ἠνεῴχθησαν αὐτῷ οἱ οὐρανοί, καὶ εἶδεν τὸ πνεῦμα τοῦ θεοῦ καταβαῖνον ὡσεὶ περιστερὰν καὶ ἐρχόμενον ἐπ' αὐτόν·
After being baptized, Jesus came up immediately from the water; and behold, the heavens were opened, and he saw the Spirit of God descending as a dove and lighting on Him (NASB).[4]

καὶ ἐκβληθέντος τοῦ δαιμονίου ἐλάλησεν ὁ κωφός
And when the demon had been cast out, the one who had been mute spoke.[5]

---

[4] Mt 3:16.
[5] Mt 9:33.

16.5 Perfect Participles

16.5.1 Perfect participles indicate a completed action with results continuing into the speaker's present. Example: "having eaten."

16.5.2 Perfect participles use the perfect tense stem with reduplication.

16.6 Perfect Active Participle

16.6.1 Table of Participle Tenses

Tense	Aug/ Red	Tense stem	TF + CV	Morpheme
Present act		pres	o	ντ/ουσα
Present mid/pas		pres	o	μενο/μενη
Aorist act		aor act	σα / o	ντ/σα
Aorist mid		aor act	σα / o	μενο/μενη
Aorist pas		aor pas	θε / ε	ντ/ισα
Perfect act	λε	perf act	κα	οτ/υια
Perfect mid/pas	*λε*	*perf pas*		*μενο/μενη*

16.6.2 Form of Perfect Active Participle

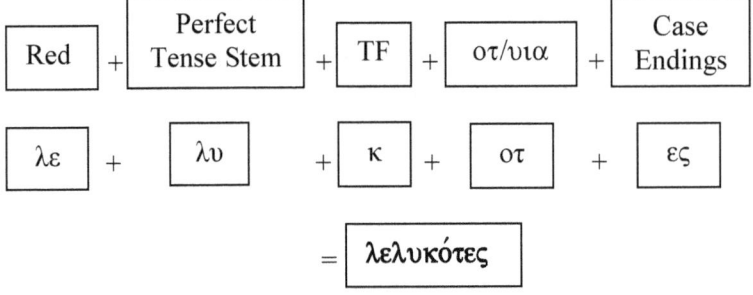

16.6.3 Perfect Active Participle Paradigm

	M	F	N
Sg Nom	λελυκώς	λελυκυῖα	λελυκός
Sg Gen	λελυκότος	λελυκυίας	λελυκότος
Sg Dat	λελυκότι	λελυκυίᾳ	λελυκότι
Sg Acc	λελυκότα	λελυκυῖαν	λελυκός
Pl Nom	λελυκότες	λελυκυῖαι	λελυκότα
Pl Gen	λελυκότων	λελυκυιῶν	λελυκότων
Pl Dat	λελυκόσι[ν]	λελυκυίαις	λελυκόσι[ν]
Pl Acc	λελυκότας	λελυκυίας	λελυκότα

Examples:

καὶ ἀπελθοῦσα εἰς τὸν οἶκον αὐτῆς εὗρεν τὸ παιδίον βεβλημένον ἐπὶ τὴν κλίνην καὶ τὸ δαιμόνιον ἐξεληλυθός.
And going back to her home, she found the child lying on the bed, the demon having left.[6]

16.7 Perfect Middle/Passive Participle

16.7.1 Table of Participle Tenses

Tense	Aug/ Red	Tense stem	TF + CV	Morpheme
Present act		pres	o	ντ/ουσα
Present mid/pas		pres	o	μενο/μενη
Aorist act		aor act	σα / ο	ντ/σα
Aorist mid		aor act	σα / ο	μενο/μενη
Aorist pas		aor pas	θε / ε	ντ/ισα
Perfect act	λε	perf act	κα	οτ/υια
Perfect mid/pas	λε	perf pas		μενο/μενη

---

[6] Mk 7:30.

16.7.2 Form of Perfect Middle/Passive Participle

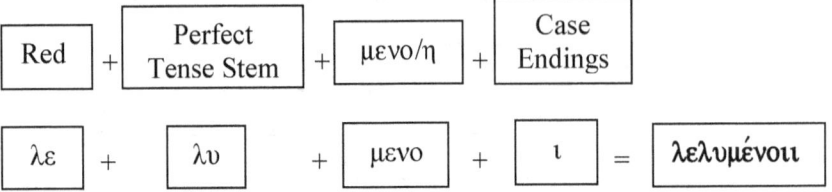

16.7.3 Perfect Middle/Passive Participle Paradigm

	M	F	N
Sg Nom	λελυμένος	λελυμένη	λελυμένον
Sg Gen	λελυμένου	λελυμένης	λελυμένου
Sg Dat	λελυμένῳ	λελυμένῃ	λελυμένῳ
Sg Acc	λελυμένον	λελυμένην	λελυμένον
Pl Nom	λελυμένοι	λελυμέναι	λελυμένα
Pl Gen	λελυμένων	λελυμένων	λελυμένων
Pl Dat	λελυμένοις	λελυμέναις	λελυμένοις
Pl Acc	λελυμένους	λελυμένας	λελυμένα

Examples:

ἵνα φανερωθῇ αὐτοῦ τὰ ἔργα ὅτι ἐν θεῷ ἐστιν εἰργασμένα.
So that his deeds may be manifested as <u>having been wrought</u> in God.[7]

---

[7] Jn 3:21.

Chapter Seventeen: Practical Applications

17 Ten Practical Applications of Knowing New Testament Greek

Introduction

Now that you have learned the basics of Koiné Greek, it's time to review some of the practical applications.

Let us first note that there are many benefits of studying *any* language. As the post-modern "linguistic turn" has shown, languages function very much as worldviews. They are not simply neutral tools to express and represent people's thoughts (a more modern view of language). Rather, languages have their own power in shaping people's ideas and therefore actions in society. Studying languages is really a study of people and peoples and the way they think; it brings us into a deep connection with human culture. Language is the foundation for communication, and communication is the foundation for distinctive human capacities.

Studying languages is also intellectually stimulating and encourages critical thought, especially about the use and meaning of words. By paying attention to grammatical and linguistic detail, students of complex languages (like Greek!) typically leave a language course with a sharper mind, which then benefits everyone else around them. Especially when a study focuses on translation, students with a knowledge of the various hazards of translation, students naturally become (at the very least) naturally better communicators and more discerning when it comes time to make decisive judgments that involve specific ideas and assertions in written form. Because it so deeply reflects and embodies human experience and even human nature, translation involves numerous dimensions of life (thought, intention, consciousness, social being, etc.), fundamental concepts (truth, deceit, relation, existence, etc.) and tasks (construction, perception, interpretation, etc.).

Finally, as one of my colleagues said, "You can't know English if you haven't learned a foreign language." That's a truism. Without something to compare to, how can we know...anything? Knowledge only works through relations. How do I know what a house is worth? I have to compare it to similar houses in a similar neighborhood at a similar time frame. How do I know what my culture is really like? I have to step outside of it by going to another country and culture. The same is true for our own language. And this is particularly the case for languages like Greek and Latin, because while they're so different on the one hand (taking us through a trip back in time), they're also the foundation for our own languages today. This makes Greek and Latin studies particularly useful.

In short, then, the benefits of learning a foreign language like Greek are rich and many.

For the rest of this chapter, ten case studies (in no particular order) will demonstrate how your new knowledge of Greek can enhance your study in important ways.

Chapter Seventeen: Practical Applications

Number 1: Identifying Plural Pronouns

As we learned, English has no second-person plural pronoun, but Greek does. The closest English equivalent is "you all" or "ya'll."[1] However, few English translations contain these renderings, and few note (usually in a footnote) all of the instances of when a plural second-person pronoun is being used in the Greek. This inevitably hides many potential insights.

Consider the serpent's use of "you" in Genesis 3:1-5 in both the Hebrew and Greek Bible. If readers depended on an ordinary English translation, it would be easy to get the impression that this conversation between the serpent and Eve was primarily between them. However, the serpent's use of "you" is plural (e.g., φάγητε and ἀποθανεῖσθε), indicates that the serpent is addressing both Adam and Eve, and that Eve is (apparently) speaking on behalf of the couple.

Or consider Matthew 6:33, "But strive first for the kingdom of God and his righteousness, and all these things will be given to you as well." The pronoun "to you" is plural (ὑμῖν). It is typical to read these words as applying to believers as individuals, but in fact Jesus is making this promise to his audience as a whole. The same goes for the well-known verse of 1 Corinthians 6:19 ("Or do you not know that your [pl] body [sg] is a temple of the Holy Spirit within you [pl], which you [pl] have from God, and that you [pl] are not your [pl] own?"), which makes for a deeper understanding of the whole church as the "temple."

---

[1] Oddly enough, "ya'll" can also function as singular; it is not uncommon to hear "ya'll" in reference to one person.

Number 2: Identifying Emphasis in Pronouns

As we learned, English translations do not utilize the tools available to them in order to consistently capture the emphasis[2] often contained in the use of personal pronouns, most notably in the phrase Ἐγώ εἰμι.[3] In a literal rendering, we would say "I I am," because the verb εἰμι is grammatically sufficient to say "I am." The addition of the first-person pronoun ἐγώ (in this case) adds emphasis to the one speaking. The most logical way of capturing this emphasis in English would be to italicize "I," so we would read "*I* am the bread of life." However, few translations use italics this way. In fact, translations typically don't even try to indicate emphasis at all. Capitalization cannot be used because "I" is already capitalized for proper punctuation. Because of appearance, underlining and bold are also off the table. Finally, because of the study required, translations rarely even make such remarks in their footnotes or marginal notes. Knowing Greek is really the best way!

The same principle goes for other pronoun uses, such as σὺ εἶ ("*you* are"),[4] ὑμεῖς ἐστε ("*you* all are"),[5] αὐτός ἐστιν ("*he* is"),[6] etc., and for other verbs. Translations simply can't capture of all this, at least not English ones.

Those with a knowledge of Greek are in a better position because they can easily identify the addition of pronouns to certain verbs. There is still another step to go in terms of knowing

---

[2] Cf. "subject focus" in Wallace, *GGBB*, 322.
[3] E.g., Jn 6:48.
[4] E.g., Matt 14:18 "...*you* are Peter..."
[5] E.g., Matt 5:13, "*You* are the salt of the earth..."
[6] E.g., Col 1:18, "*He* is the head of the body, the church..."

if the pronoun is used for emphasis and if so, what *kind* of emphasis ("contrast," "subjective focus," etc.). However, this discussion cannot even take place if readers are unaware of what words are actually being used.

Number 3: Identifying Different Words

There is often more than one English equivalent for one Greek word, and often more than one Greek equivalent for one English word. This means that there is rarely a strict one-for-one correspondence between certain Greek and English words. Sometimes, for significant words, English translations will vow to be consistent in certain renderings (in the "Preface to the Reader" or "Translator's Introduction"). For instance, in most English Bibles, the Hebrew term for *Yahweh* (יהוה) is always rendered as "Lord" in all caps ("LORD"), or "Lord God." This way, English readers can always know that a certain Hebrew word is used—and not alternatives like *El* or *Elohim* ("God"). But, most of the time, there is not such an easy clue of knowing what original term is used.

For example, what is the word for "have/exercise authority" in the ESV and NRSV rendering of 1 Timothy 2:12? Is it ἐξουσιάζω? Κυριεύω? προΐστημι? ἔχειν ἐξουσίαν? No, it's none of these. The term is αὐθεντέω, which is used nowhere else in the Greek OT or Greek NT, and it cannot simply be assumed to mean an ordinary use or neutral exercise of authority like some of these other terms.[7]

---

[7] See Jamin Hübner, "Revisiting αὐθεντέω in 1 Tim. 2:12: What Does the Extant Data Really Show?" *JSPL* 4:3 (Spring 2015): 41-69; Jamin Hübner, "Translating αὐθεντέω (*authenteō*) in 1 Timothy 2:12," *Priscilla Papers* 29:2 (Spring 2015): 16-26.

Or consider the English verb "love," which can be translated from ἀγαπάω or φιλέω, which may (or may not) have different shades of meaning. Without knowing Greek, it is difficult knowing which term is used. This is, in fact, why English concordances can be misleading: they are not necessarily organized according to Greek and Hebrew terms, but instead according to English word occurences. So, for example, if one was to look up "love" in these kinds of concordances, both Matthew 23:6 and Matthew 24:12 would be listed even though they are completely different Greek terms. This is obviously potentially (though not necessarily) misleading, and it highlights the importance of using a Greek-English concordance or Greek lexicon when identifying the occurences of certain terms.

Number 4: Identifying Words that Aren't There

As we learned, translators often have to supply words that are not found in the Greek text in order to retain proper English grammar. Without knowing Greek, it is not clear what English words directly reflect Greek words and what English words are supplied by translators.

Consider John 3:16, "For God so loved the world that he gave his only Son, so that everyone who believes in him may not perish but may have eternal life." The phrase "everyone who" or "whosoever believes" is πᾶς ὁ πιστεύων, literally, "all the believing ones." The difference between saying "whosoever" or "anyone" and "all the believing ones" may be significant (especially for those embroiled in theological debates about "total depravity"); Jesus is not saying anything about the capacity of those who do not believe, but is simply talking about what *will* happen to those who *do* believe.

As another case in point, Ephesians 5:22 reads, "Wives, be subject to your husbands as you are to the Lord." As crazy as it sounds to many evangelical Christians, the word "be subject" or "submit" doesn't exist in the verse; it reads Αἱ γυναῖκες τοῖς ἰδίοις ἀνδράσιν ὡς τῷ κυρίῳ. Why, then, do translators insert "submit"? Because v. 22 depends on v. 21 for its verb: "Be subject to one another out of reverence for Christ...women, [submitting] to your husbands as to the Lord." This means that v. 22 depends upon v. 21 contextually and syntactically. Hence the NLT rendering, "submit to one another out of reverence for Christ. For wives, this means..." Likewise, Lexham's *Syntactical Greek New Testament* places v. 22 is a "segment clause" placed underneath the "sentence" of v. 21.

After reading this passage in Greek, it is obvious that it is a terrible mistake for Bible publishers and editors to insert a paragraph break (and/or heading) between Ephesians 5:21 and 5:22. The ESV, for instance, has both a paragraph break and a new heading (as does the NASB, HSCB, NET, and NKJV), creating the impression that the command for wives to submit to husbands (or, some concept of "headship") has little to do with the mutual submission of the previous verse. The KJV, RSV, NRSV, NIV (2011), NLT, NCV, MSG, TLB, NLV, AMP, CEB, GNT, VOICE and others rightly do not do this, because splitting up the two verses is not grammatically warranted.

If theologians had also been biblical scholars throughout church history, perhaps most Christians for the past several centuries would not have interpreted Ephesians 5:22 in isolation from 5:21. But since this has unfortunately not been the case, many Christians continue to make arguments on the basis of 5:21 without realizing that the word "submit" isn't there, and refers back to something very different than what they think (or thought) it means.

In the same theological area, 1 Corinthians 11:10 in the NRSV reads, "a woman ought to have a symbol of authority on her head, because of the angels." The word "symbol of" is not in the Greek text. It simply has ἡ γυνὴ ἐξουσίαν ἔχειν ἐπὶ τῆς κεφαλῆς, or, "a woman ought to have authority on her head." Translators insert "a symbol of" for a variety of reasons (some cultural, some theological), but in doing so distorts its meaning—suggesting that man's authority (symbolized by some head-covering), and not woman's authority, is being talked about. But as Gordon Fee has noted, "there is no known evidence either that exousia is ever taken in this passive sense [103 NT occurrences, Philo, LXX, Josephus] or that the idiom 'to have authority over' ever refers to an external authority different from the subject of the sentence."[8] Thus, as another commentator notes, "The woman's head is not one over which others have authority. God has granted her

---

[8] Gordon Fee, *The First Epistle to the Corinthians*, NICNT (Grand Rapids: Eerdmans, 2013), 574. Cf. Roy Ciampa and Brian Rosner, *The First Letter to the Corinthians*, PNTC (Grand Rapids: Eerdmans, 2010), 533; David E. Garland, *1 Corinthians*, BCENT (Grand Rapids: Eerdmans, 2003), 524-526; John Frame, *The Doctrine of the Christian Life* (Phillipsburg: Presbyterian and Reformed, 2008), 629; Leon Morris, 1 Corinthians, TNTC (Downers Grove: InterVarsity, 2008), 152; ; C. K. Barrett, *A Commentary on the First Epistle to the Corinthians* (London: A. & C. Black, 1968), 250; F. F. Bruce, *1 &2 Corinthians*, New Century Bible (Greenwood: Attic, 1971), 106; James Hurley, "Did Paul Require Veils or the Silence of Women?" *WTJ* 35 (Winter 1973): 206-12; Kenneth Bailey, *Paul Through Mediterranean Eyes: Cultural Studies in 1 Corinthians 11* (Downers Grove: InterVarsity Academic, 2011), 301-313.

authority to pray and prophesy. She exercises that authority in a dignified way by respecting both herself and the rest of the congregation through the avoidance of provocative attire or any dress or behavior which would bring shame on herself, others, or God…"[9] In other words, Paul's point is the *opposite* of what most interpreters throughout history have traditionally thought.

In many cases like these, the NASB, which italicizes words not present in the Greek, can be very helpful. Using the same example from above, the NASB reads, "Therefore the woman ought to have *a symbol of* authority on her head, because of the angels." Of course, it would have been better not to even have "a symbol of" at all, but putting it in italics is better than nothing.

Number 5: Identifying Words that *Should* Be There

Translations not only supply words that aren't found in the Greek, but eliminate words that *are*.

Consider the NIV's rendering of εὐθύς in Mark 1:21 and 31: it's not there! This is probably because the translators expected context to provide the temporal sense of time/urgency, or because Mark is notorious for using the word so many times in his short Gospel (41 of 59 in the NT), so, since "we all get the point," why bother translating this word again? Whatever the case, no attempt was made to translate the term.

Or consider the conjunction δὲ, which is typically rendered "now," "so then," or "in turn." In 1 Timothy 2:12, the term is completely untranslated in the ESV, NRSV, NIV, and NLT (in contrast with the NASB, NET, and KJV). This is an unfortunate

---

[9] Ciampa and Rosner, *The First Letter to the Corinthians*, 533.

mistake, because it gives the impression that verse 12 may be disconnected from verse 11 when, in fact, they are logically connected. The author's train of thought about women's (or wives') demeanor and specific behaviors continues to be addressed in verse 12, not cut off by an introduction to the new topic of generic Christian ministries. There are many other cases like this.

Number 6: Knowing What Text Should (and Shouldn't) be There

Although this point is not directly addressed in this grammar, it is one of the benefits of learning Greek in concert with textual criticism: having the ability to discern what verses and words were most likely in the earliest forms of the New Testament and what verses and words were later additions and revisions.

Consider John 5:4. No matter what copy of the Bible one has (with the exception of the KJV/NKJV), the text jumps from 5:3 to 5:5. This is because the verse was a later addition to the text of John, but the chapter and verse numbering of the Bible (between the 900s and 1200s AD) came before this discovery. So, while it looks as it John 5:4 was *recently erased*, in fact, it was *added long-ago*. The same goes for Matthew 17:21, 18:11, 23:14; Mark 7:16, 9:44, 9:46, 11:26, 15:28, 16:9–20; Luke 17:36, 23:17; John 5:3–4, 7:53-8:11; Acts 8:37, 15:34, 24:6–7, 28:29; and Romans 16:24.

Having a knowledge of Greek and textual criticism allows one to understand why there are differences in translation, because many differences are due to the source texts being used ("textual variation") and not the translation itself.

Chapter Seventeen: Practical Applications

Number 7: Identifying Emphasis from Double-Negatives

Two negatives in Greek equals one big negative. οὐ (not) + μή (not) = οὐ μή (very not!). But without knowing Greek, it's impossible to know where this happens. This is especially true since English translations are terribly inconsistent in their renderings of this "negative concord" couplet.

The phrase οὐ μή (used 94 times in the NT) is sometimes translated with emphasis ("never," "may it never be," "by no means," etc.) but not at other times (simply rendered, "not"). For example, the NRSV and ESV renders Matthew 5:20 as "For I tell you, unless your righteousness exceeds that of the scribes and Pharisees, you will *never* enter the kingdom of heaven," (cf. NIV, "certaintly not") and 5:26 as "you will *never* get out until you have paid the last penny." Despite these appropriate renderings, there is no emphasis in the same translations in Matthew 10:42, "none of these will lose their reward," even though the same words οὐ μή is there. The NIV in this verse correctly has, "*certaintly not* lose their reward."

Or consider Hebrews 8:11, "And they shall not teach, each one his neighbor" (ESV). The NET more accurately has, "And there will be no need *at all* for each one to teach." The same goes for Romans 4:8, which the NET and NIV rightly has "will *never* count sin"; virtually all other translations do not attempt to capture this emphasis. But, then we're left asking: why aren't the same translations (the NET and NIV) consistent in its rendering of οὐ μή elsewhere, like in Galatians 5:16?

In 1 Thessalonians 4:15, the NRSV and NIV rightly emphasizes the phrase οὐ μὴ φθάσωμεν τοὺς κοιμηθέντας· ("will *by no means* precede" in NRSV; "will *certainly not* precede" in NIV). Oddly, the NASB and ESV lacks any emphasis. And oddly, again, in Revelation 21:27, the NRSV is one of the only translations to *not* emphasize the double-negative!

As you can tell, virtually no translation consistently brings out the emphasis of the double-negative οὐ μή. It is difficult to tell why, since it is extremely easy to do and there is little reason not to. Nevertheless, reading the Greek once again shows the way.

Number 8: Identifying "Woman/Wife" and "Man/Husband"

As we learned, Greek has no clear grammatical way of consistently distinguishing between "woman" and "wife" or "man" and "husband." The same two terms are used. This leaves it up the translators to decide whether the author is talking specifically about a married person or not when using γυνή or ἀνήρ. Of course, by choosing the broader category of "man" and "woman," translators largely leave it up to readers to decide if a husband or wife is specifically being addressed or not.

It is fairly obvious, for example, that the "Canaanite γυνή" in Matthew 15:22 is speaking of a woman and not necessarily a wife. Thus, all English translations have "woman." Similarly, in Matthew 5:21, it is obvious that "who divorces his γυνή" is speaking of a wife, and not a generic woman. Interestingly, translations do not necessarily consistently translate these terms when the sense is rather clear. For example, the NRSV has "man" instead of "husband" in Mark 10:2 ("Is it lawful for a *man* to divorce his wife...").

In other cases, the meaning is not so easy to discern, such as 1 Timothy 2 and 1 Corinthians 11. Appealing to statistics is not always helpful; the general trend of translations is towards a generic over a marital rendering, but this is only a trend.[10] It is thus "safe" to assume a generic rendering until shown otherwise, but, again, one cannot simply make an argument for a marital rendering because one translation contains it.

Number 9: Experiencing Phonetic Effect

Much of the Bible was meant to be read outloud, not read quietly in private. This includes much or most of the New Testament. Various aspects of communication is therefore lost when moving into a different language, such as how a text *sounds*, including its cadence/rhythm, syllabic structure, and overall effect.

Ephesians 1:3-14 is a single sentence in Greek, making it one of the longest sentences in the whole Bible. As a person reads all 200+ words, it is easy to feel the weight of the doxology the Apostle is creating. He goes on and on about God, grace, and salvation. Translations cut up this sentence into three or four sentences for easier reading. Without knowing Greek, this run-on sentence would remain hidden, and its full effect would not be felt.

---

[10] The NRSV, for instance, renders γυνή generically as "woman/women" 162 times, and specifically as "wife/wives" 76 times in the NT; ἀνήρ 104 times generically, and maritally 48 times.

Consider also this phrase in the Lord's Prayer (Matthew 6:9-10):

hallowed be your name. (6 syllables)
Your kingdom come. (4 syllables)
Your will be done, (4 syllables)

Only the last two sentences seem to flow together, each starting with "your" and ending with the same vowel sound (in "come" and "done"). In Greek, however, we read this:

ἁγιασθήτω τὸ ὄνομά σου, (10 syllables)
ἐλθέτω ἡ βασιλεία σου, (9 syllables)
γενηθήτω τὸ θέλημά σου, (9 syllables)

Notice that the first word of each phrase ends with the same sound (*oh*) and last word of each phrase ends with the same sound and same word (*soo*). Also notice that each phrase is made of four words. All of this is lost in translation, and so its overall audible effect is diminished.[11] There are many other examples like these (e.g., Phil 2:5-11).

Number 10: Keeping Theology at Bay

Learning Greek (or Hebrew) is central to becoming a biblical scholar, and biblical study limits (among other things) the bounds of theology (especially systematics).

---

[11] Although, interestingly, the English somehow managed to retain the decreasing number of syllables in the phrases, at least generally.

Chapter Seventeen: Practical Applications

For as long as the disciplines have been alive, there has always been a debate between the "biblical studies department" and the "theology department." As it has often been characterized, the theologian draws conclusions from the text that causes the biblical scholar to say "you can't say that, that's taking it out of context!", and the biblical scholar draws conclusions from the text that causes the theologian to say "you can't say that; that's heresy!" And so it is in the advantage of the biblical scholar to know more thoroughly and deeply the "world of the text."[12]

Being saturated in such a world, the biblical scholar is able to see theological trends and movements for what they are: trends and movements. She can resist the tyranny of certain strands of Christianity that demand assent to temporal theological formulations that may or may not have any bearing on the world of the text, the gospel of the New Testament, and the Jesus of the Gospels. As Marshall puts it,

> The later development of creeds and systematic theology is a continuation of [a] process that can never come to an end...the New Testament writers go behind the apostolic deposit to combat error and to find *fresh ways of expressing the gospel.* Orthodoxy is not tied to specific vocabularies and forms of words.[13]

---

[12] The best introductions to that "world" of the New Testament text have already been cited in the introduction under "summer reading."

[13] I. Howard Marshall, *Moving Beyond the Bible to Theology* (Grand Rapids: Baker Academic, 2004), 72. Cf. Sallie McFague, *Models of God* (Minneapolis: Fortress Press, 1987) and especially, her *Metaphorical Theology* (Minneapolis: Fortress Press, 1982).

One of the worst and most enticing forms of idolatry is *linguistic* idolatry. Symbolic systems can become far too sacred—precisely because they *are* so meaningful—so that they become a tool of oppression.

Biblical scholarship is that life-giving process of continuous cultivation, like a gardener tending each row each season, rotating crops at spring time with new seeds and adding new topsoil—all on the same plot of land with the same set of tools. Genuine biblical study breaks up the hard soil of stale theological jargon that has lost its meaning in an ever-changing world. It gives life to dead metaphors. It dares to explore how the world of the text might be significant and meaningful today[14]—all without falling into the hands of ideologies that have lost a sense of vision and hope.[15]

Knowing Greek brings both humility and competence when it comes to biblical study and theology. Both are crucial to the health of the church, of society, and the renewal of the world.

---

[14] Some of the best work being cultivated in this area today comes from biblical scholars like N. T. Wright, John Goldingay, J. Richard Middleton and others, as well as from preachers, ethicists, and philosophers like Fleming Rutledge, Stanley Hauerwas, James K. A. Smith, et al. The most relevant organizations in this field are probably the Canadian-American Theological Association (CATA), the Institute for Biblical Research (IBR), and (less frequently) select study groups of the American Academy of Religion (AAR) and Society of Biblical Literature (SBL).

[15] For a radical vision of how Christian symbols, words, and ideas might be completely reconstructed for the next century, see Gordon Kaufman, *In Face of Mystery: A Constructive Theology* (Cambridge: Harvard University Press, 1993) and Sallie McFague, *The Body of God: An Ecological Theology* (Minneapolis: Fortress Press, 1993). For a more orthodox and conservative proposal, see Kevin Vanhoozer, *The Drama of Doctrine* (Louisville: Westminster John Knox, 2005) and Daniel Migliore, *Faith Seeking Understanding* (Grand Rapids: Eerdmans, 2014).

Grammatical Glossary

Abbreviations of Sources

GGBB = *Greek Grammar Beyond the Basics* (Wallace)
Fundamentals = *Fundamentals of New Testament Greek* (Porter et. al.)
Reading = *Reading Koiné Greek* (Decker)
MW = *Merriam Webster's Online Dictionary*

accusative (acc.): "the case of *extent*, or *limitation*....It is primarily used to limit the action of a verb as to extent, direction, or goal" (*GGBB*, 178).

active (act.): "...in the active voice the subject *performs, produces,* or *experiences the action* or *exists* in the *state* expressed by the verb" (*GGBB*, 178).

adjective (adj.): "...a modifier of a noun or other substantive" (*GGBB*, 292).

adverb (adv.): "...words that modify or describe verbs" (*Reading*, 105).

aorist (aor.): "The aorist simply refers to a situation in summary without indicating anything further about the action" (*Reading*, 120); "...the aorist tense-form depicts the event from the standpoint of the speaker or writer as a complete event" (*Fundamentals*, 39).

anarthrous: without the article.

article (art.): "...the article intrinsically has the ability to *conceptualize*...the article is able to turn just about any part of speech into a noun and, therefore, a concept...it is used predominately to stress the identity of an individual or class or quality" (*GGBB*, 209).

articular: with the article.

aspect: "Verbal aspect is, in general, the portrayal of the action (or state) as to its *progress, results,* or *simple occurrence*" (*GGBB*, 499); "Aspect is the category that tells us how the author portrays the situation (as a whole, as a process, or as a state)" (*Reading*, 223); "The primary category of Greek verb usage, namely, the speaker's or writer's perspective on the action of the verb; aspect is expressed by the selection of a particular tense-form" (*Fundamentals*, 33).

case: "…indicates the basic relationship of a noun, pronoun, or adjective to other elements of a sentence" (*Fundamentals*, 22).

cognate (cog.): "3a) related by descent from the same ancestral language; 3b) of a word or morpheme: related by derivation, borrowing, or descent; 3)c of a substantive: related to a verb usually by derivation and serving as its object to reinforce the meaning" (*MW*).

conjugation: "a schematic arrangement of the inflectional forms of a verb" (*MW*); cf. "declensions."

conjunction: "a type of particle (i.e., a word that has a single form) used to join grammatical unites, including words, phrases, clauses, and paragraphs" (*Fundamentals*, 170).

continous aspect ("imperfective"): "One of the three verbal aspects in Greek…it views the action of the verb as being in progress. The speaker or writer expresses this aspect by selecting the present (or the imperfect) tense-form" (*Fundamentals*, 54).

contract verbs: "verbs whose stem ends in a, e, or o, vowels that 'contract,' or combine, with the connecting vowel or ending in the present and imperfect tense-forms" (*Fundamentals*, 170).

dative (dat.): "…the case of *personal interest, reference/respect* (pure dative), *position* (locative), and *means* (instrumental)…when the dative is used of persons, it speaks about the one(s) concerned about (or affected by) the action; when it is used of things, it addresses the *framework* in which an act occurs" (*GGBB*, 139).

declensions: "grouping of nouns on the basis of their word formation" (*Fundamentals*, 16).

Grammatical Glossary

definite (def.): "3) typically designating an identified or immediately identifiable person or thing <the definite article the>" (*MW*).

demonstrative (dem.): "2) pointing out the one referred to and distinguishing it from others of the same class <demonstrative pronouns>" (*MW*).

digamma (*waw* or *wau*): an archaic letter of the Greek alphabet (ϝ) that came after epsilon. It was originally called *waw* or *wau*, with a /w/ sound, and principally remained in use as the numeral six.

enclitic: "a word that does not normally take its own accent because it is read closely with the preceding word, which provides for its accentuation" (*Fundamentals*, 13).

feminine: see "gender."

future (fut.): "does not clearly convey verbal aspect…It is best described as conveying a sense of *expectation*" (*Fundamentals*, 86); "The future-tense form expresses expectation, which is most commonly rendered in English as future time….The Greek future tense-form is probably best viewed as aspectually vague. That is, from the form alone it is not possible to say that the writer is viewing the situation either as a process, as a complete event, or as a state" (*Reading*, 309-10); "With reference to *aspect*, the future seems to offer an *external* portrayal, something of a temporal counterpart to the aorist indicative…Our view that the future is both a true aspect and an exclusively external one is based both on morphology and usage: Its formal link to the aorist suggests that it shares its aspect with the aorist (analogous to the imperfect sharing its aspect with the present, and the pluperfect with the perfect). This would make it a summary tense" (*GGBB*, 566-67).

gender: "…refers to the differentiation of nouns and adjectives into three groups, or patterns, labeled *masculine, feminine,* and *neuter*" (*Fundamentals*, 23).

genitive (gen.): "A genitive-case noun functions to restrict (or *modify*) another word in the sentence, usually the word directly preceeding it in word order" (*Reading*, 47).

gloss: "…is a simple English equivalent of the lexical form without necessarily considering the context. It is *not* a translation of the inflected form" (*Reading*, 38).

indicative (ind.): "One of the four moods of Greek verbs (the others: subjective, optative, and imperative), used to make an assertion or raise a questions about what is assumed to be reality" (*Fundamentals*, 34); "The indicative mood is, in general, the mood of assertion, or *presentation of certainty*" (*GGBB*, 448).

indefinite (indef.): "not definite: as a) typically designating an unidentified, generic, or unfamiliar person or thing <the indefinite articles a and an> <indefinite pronouns>" (*MW*).

infinitive (inf.): "Frequently called a verbal noun, this form of the verb expresses aspect (through its tense-form) and voice, but not person or number. It performs a variety of verbal and substantival functions" (*Fundamentals*, 34);

intransitive: "Verbs that do not have a direct object…'Her diamond sparkled.' " (*Reading*, 77).

imperfect (impf.): "the imperfect mirrors the present tense both in its general aspect [continuous] and its specific uses (the only difference being, for the most part, that the imperfect is used for past time)" (*GGBB*, 541).

imperative (impv.): "is used to direct someone's actions and consequently is frequently used in commands ('go' or 'let them go')" (*Fundamentals*, 41).

koiné: "a dialect or language of a region that has become the common or standard language of a larger area" (*MW*).

Koiné: "the Greek language commonly spoken and written in eastern Mediterranean countries in the Hellenistic and Roman periods" (*MW*).

masculine (masc.): see "gender."

manuscript (ms. and mss.): identifies the physical copies of the Greek NT that contain the given reading.

mood: "A feature of the Greek verb that describes the speaker's or writer's attitude toward the relation of the verbal action to reality" (*Fundamentals*, 34).

noun (n.): "a word that is used to indicate some thing or concept, whether as a particular instancve or as a class of items" (*Fundamentals*, 19); "a word that is the name of something (such as a person, animal, place, thing, quality, idea, or action) and is typically used in a sentence as subject or object of a verb or as object of a preposition" (*MW*).

nominative (nom.): "the case of designation or naming,,,often used to indicate the subject of the sentence" (*Fundamentals*, 22).

object (obj.):

objective: "used for the direct object; it identifies who or what receives the action of the verb" (*Reading*, 32).

oblique: non-nominative.

particle: undeclinable words (words that don't have the endings of any declension), such as preopositions, conjunctions, and adverbs.

passive (pass.): "conveys the idea that someone or something, whether explicitly identified or not, is acting on the grammatical subject" (*Fundamentals*, 141).

person (pers.): "The three 'roles' that Greek identifies involving the speaker/writer and others in the action of the verb" (*Fundamentals*, 34).

perfect (pf.): "the perfect tense is used to depict an action or event as representing a complex state of affairs and hence is said to convey stativ verbal aspect...the perfect tense does not primarily refer to the time when an event occurs but can be used to speak of past, present, and even occasionally future actions" (*Fundamentals* 319).

perfective ("completive aspect"): "One of the three verbal asepcts in Greek...it views the action of the verb as a complete whole. The speaker or writer expresses this aspect by selecting the aorist tense-form" (*Fundamentals*, 33).

possessive (poss.): "The substantive in the gentive possesses the thing to which it stands related. That is, in some sense the head noun is owned by the genitive noun" (*GGBB*, 81).

post-positive (ppos.): "conjunctions [that] occur only after the first word or element of a clause" (*Fundamentals*, 181).

preposition (prep.): "particles, or undeclinable words (i.e., they do not take endings), that specify and enhance the case meanings of substantives (such as nouns)...the whole group of words is called a prepositional phrase" (*Fundamentals*, 132).

present (pres.): "represents an activity as in process (or in progress)...usually present time, but it may be other than or broader than the present time" (*GGBB*, 514).

pronoun (pron.): "a word that stands in the place of another element in a language" (*Fundamentals*, 96).

participle (ptc.): "frequently called a verbal adjective, is a verb form that has characteristics of an adjuctive in that it has gender, case, and number, but also characteristics of a verb, in that it has aspect and voice. The participle, a marvelously flexible form, can function as a modifier, a substantive, or a verb. Often '-ing' is used to translate the participle, as in '<u>running</u> from the house, he disappeared.') (*Fundamentals*, 41).

Grammatical Glossary

reflexive (reflex.): "of, relating to, or constituting an action (as in "he perjured himself") directed back on the agent or the grammatical subject" (*MW*).

reflexive pronoun: "a word used to 'reflect' the action of the agent back upon the agent (e.g., 'he surprised <u>himself</u>')" (*Fundamentals*, 279).

reciprocal pronoun: "a word (occurring only in the plural) that expresses a mutual relationship or among elements in a group (e.g., 'they trusted <u>each other</u>'" (*Fundamentals*, 279).

simple aspect ("stative"): "One of the three verbal aspects in Greek…it views the action as reflecting a given (often complex) state of affairs. The speaker or writer expresses this aspect by selecting the perfect (also plurperfect) tense-form" (*Fundamentals*, 315).

substantive: a word of word group that functions as a noun or pronoun.

subjunctive (sub.): "The subjunctive mood is used to express a projected realm that may at some time exist and may even now exist, but that is held up for consideration simply as projection of the speaker's or writer's mind" (*Fundamentals*, 155).

subject (subj.): the person or thing that experiences or performs the action of the verb.

suffix (suff.): "an affix occurring at the end of a word, base, or phrase — compare" (*MW*).

tense-form: "The means in Greek for conveying the speaker's or writer's choice of verbal aspect" (*Fundamentals*, 33).

transitive: "a verb that takes a direct object…'She *drove* the *car* to the mall' " (*Reading*, 77).

voice: "A feature of the Greek verb that describes the relation of the grammatical subject to the cause of the action of the verb" (*Fundamentals*, 34).

www.ingramcontent.com/pod-product-compliance
Lightning Source LLC
Chambersburg PA
CBHW070325230426
43663CB00011B/2217